Short and Sweet
Takes the Fifth

COMPILED AND EDITED
BY SUSAN CHEEVES KING

GRACE
PUBLISHING

Broken Arrow, OK

Royalties for this book are donated to World Christian Broadcasting.

SHORT AND SWEET TAKES THE FIFTH

ISBN-13: 978-1-60495-049-6

TABLE OF CONTENTS

Introduction 5

1. Crowns and Robes *Jorja Davis* 9
2. The Plane Trips from Hades *Reba Rhyne* 12
3. In the Deep Woods *Karen Allen* 16
4. Treason of the Heart *Paul Aaron Hinton* 20
5. The Mysterious Man *Jewell Utt* 25
6. One Thing of Note *Joylene M. Bailey* 28
7. The Story in the Storm *Sara Hague* 31
8. Fear *Toni Armstrong Sample* 34
9. Just My Luck *Laura Luptowski Seeley* 37
10. Patty and Me *Lin Daniels* 39
11. God Will Lead *Steve Duke* 41
12. Mom's New Pet *Heidi Gaul* 43
13. Finding Scot *Pamela Groupe Groves* 47
14. Fall in Texas *Leah Hinton* 48
15. Bird Taxi Me *Lisa Worthey Smith* 52
16. Oh, to Have Seen Him! *Charles Huff* 54
17. Old News *Penny Hunt* 56
18. Pope Gregory and the War Tribe *Tom Kennedy* 59
19. The Road Ahead *Liz Kimmel* 63
20. In the Dark *Susan Thogerson Maas* 66
21. Beatlemania – Indianapolis, 1964 *Darlene S. Mackey* 68
22. The Plaza *Michael Reynolds* 71
23. Play It Again *Jeanetta Chrystie* 73
24. Howler *Debra Pierce* 76
25. Angel Falls *Ken Proctor* 79
26. Same Train, Same Seat, Same View *Andrea Woronick* 82
27. Soap Opera Story *Alice Murray* 84
28. Thank you, Jesus and Pancho Villa! *Susanna Shutz Robar* 87
29. Back the Way We Came *Frank Ramirez* 91

30. ONE DARK NIGHT *Angela Mattingly* 92

31. STORY THIEF *David Shorts* 95

32. GHOST *Pamela Rosales* 97

33. COMMUNING WITH THE DEAD *Sharon Cook* 102

34. CHILLS *E.V. Sparrow* 104

35. A WRECK WITH A VAN AND A BOAT *Randy Swanson* 108

36. THE LIE *Tabitha Abel* 110

37. A FISH TALE *Nicey Eller* 113

38. THE THIN PLACE *Patricia Huey* 117

39. THE DAIRY QUEENS' SWEET REVENGE *Kenneth Avon White* 121

40. BUSY IN THE NIGHT *Mary Hunt Webb* 126

41. THE BOY *Jenny Calvert* 128

42. THE FIRST LIBRARY *Jacinta S. Fontenelle* 130

43. A MONTH OF GOOD DEEDS *Kelly Pankratz* 134

44. MINISTERING ANGELS *Dottie Lovelady Rogers* 138

45. MY MOTHER, THE SPEEDSTER *Lanita Boyd* 141

46. ABOUT THE AUTHORS 143

INTRODUCTION

I t all started decades ago when Mary Lou Redding caught an idea from a professor at Fort Wayne University. Further inspired by Joseph A. Ecclesine's "Big Words Are for the Birds" (at the end of the Introduction), she started assigning a one-syllable-word exercise in classes she taught at various writers' conferences all over the country.

Over the past twenty years, I have continued giving this assignment to those in my own classes. Writers at these conferences are motivated to learn whatever I can teach them about perfecting their craft because they know they're going to apply what they've learned, probably within an hour after they leave the classroom.

Still, they have come with the attitude that we who love to write all share. After all, we're writers. We love words. If a few words are good, many are better — especially the interesting word, maybe the elegant word…and definitely the special word only a particular writer can use.

And we do love to use the long, impressive words. But that can work against good communication. The truth is, the best communication is what the readers/listeners understand with the least effort — a Mr. Spock mind meld as it were — as if the ideas are just flowing from the writer's mind to theirs with no actual words involved.

We may love words, but if we use too many of them and ones that are not familiar and comfortable to the average reader/listener, then words just get in the way. Writing tight (saying a lot with a little) and using crisp, clear, accessible words in our writing and speech bring joy to the readers/listeners even if they may not know why.

That's good news for any of us who long for others to understand us, to hear us. The words we really should be using most of the time are already known to us. We don't have to get a college degree to learn them; we just think that we do. So we all need to break our attachments to those multi-syllable aliens that even non-professional writers/speakers tend to favor and get back to the simple words of our childhood.

Here is the basic assignment followed by the writers in each book in the *Short and Sweet* series:

Choose something you're passionate about, something that's important to you. Then write about it in 250-550 words, using words of only one syllable. We are accepting non-fiction, fiction, and poetry submissions.

Six exceptions:

1. Any proper noun is okay. (Don't lie. If you were born in California, don't write Maine; if a name is Machenheimer, don't write Clark.)
2. You may use polysyllabic words of 5 letters or fewer — for example: into, over, area, about
3. You may use contractions of more than one syllable such as couldn't, wouldn't, didn't
4. You may use numbers (even those that are polysyllabic).
5. As in any published work, direct quotes must be rendered word-for-word as they appear in the original, so their wording is exempt from the rules. This includes verses from the Bible — but only translations, not paraphrases (such as The Message).
6. Words for family (for which there are no one-syllable synonyms) are fine: mother, father, sister, brother, sibling, husband, daughter, cousin, nephew, family.

If you're a writer — or aspire to be — and this assignment intrigues you, why not give it a try? If you contact me at shortandsweettoo@gmail.com, I will send you the upcoming theme and deadline. You could be seeing your own work featured in the next book in the Short and Sweet series.

To learn which of these stories are fiction or non-fiction, go to grace-publishing.com, select About Us, then scroll down to select Short and Sweet Takes the Fifth's Answers.

Susan Cheeves King

Big Words Are for the Birds
Joseph A. Ecclesine

When you come right down to it, there is no law that says you have to use big words in ads.

There are lots of small words, and good ones, that can be made to say all the things you want to say — quite as well as the big ones.

It may take more time to find the small words — but it can be well worth it. For most small words are quick to grasp. And best of all, most of us know what they mean.

Some small words — a lot of them, in fact — can say a thing just the way it should be said. They can be crisp, brief, to the point. Or they can be soft, round, smooth — rich with just the right feel, the right taste.

Use them with care and what you say can be slow or fast to read — as you wish.

Small words have a charm all their own — the charm of the quick, the lean, the lithe, the light on their toes. They dance, twist, turn, sing — light the way for the eyes of those who read, like sparks in the night — and stay on to sing some more.

Small words are clean, the grace notes of prose. There is an air to them that leaves you with the keen sense that they could not be more clear.

You know what they say the way you know a day is bright and fair — at first sight. And you find as you read that you like the way they say it.

Small words are sweet — to the ear, the tongue, and the mind.

Small words are gay — and lure you to their song as the flame lures the moth (which is not a bad thing for an ad to do).

Small words have a world of their own — a big world in which all of us live most of the time (which makes it a good place for ads, too).

And small words can catch big thoughts and hold them up for all who read to see — like bright stones in rings of gold.

With a good stock of small words, and the will to use them, you can write ads that will do all you want your ads to do — and more, much more.

In fact, if you play your cards right, you can write ads the way they all say ads should be done: in words like these (all the way down to the last one, that, is) of just one syllable.

Joseph A. Ecclesine was a Madison Avenue copywriter in the *Mad Men* era. He originally wrote this piece in the 1960s for other copywriters.

A shorter version titled "Words of One Syllable," ran in *Reader's Digest*.

These two versions have also appeared in various other publications while being used as inspirational models for college writing courses around the country.

Born in Boston, Ecclesine

graduated from Fordham University in 1929, months before the stock market crash that triggered the Great Depression. He was fortunate to find work at the *Bronx Home News* during that period. He later worked in the press department of NBC in Manhattan, where he met his future wife, Margy, also a writer there.

They celebrated more than 50 years of marriage and had eight children. While living in New York, he worked at several major ad agencies and became promotion director of *Look Magazine*.

His catchy headlines and prose could be found in the campaigns of numerous companies, including IBM, National Geographic, Revlon and American Airlines. He also wrote fiction and essays, with a 1930s piece in *Esquire* magazine, followed by work in *The New Yorker, Newsweek* and *Short Story International*. He had an innate curiosity about everything, which translated into an extreme zest for life.

An accomplished watercolorist, Ecclesine allegedly sold his first piece to boxer Gene Tunney, who held the world heavyweight championship in the late 1920s. Ecclesine's watercolors were featured in *The Artist* magazine, and he had a one-man show during his retirement in San Diego. While living in California during his final years, he taught courses in memoir writing for senior citizens in a continuing education program at UCSD (University of California at San Diego).

1

CROWNS AND ROBES

Jorja Davis

O ver the years we moved often due to my husband's job. From Texas to Florida, from Florida to Alaska, from Alaska to Illinois, from Illinois to Washington, from Washington to Germany, from Germany to Texas, from Texas to Georgia. Over the years and moves, I kept bits of my born-and-bred Texas drawl. Lots of flat-tongued schwas, equal sounds from one part of a word to the next, and I even give one-part words two or more sounds. To this day, I often say *ca'-uht* for *cat, Chriz'-muhs* for *Christmas, cra' yon* for *crown, 'uh'-fah-r* for *afar, 'warsh'- rag* for *wash'-cloth*. My husband's name is said Bee-uhl not Bill. I've been told it's lazy talk. When I talk to Mama on the phone or when I'm stressed, all words get flat and long. It makes short and sweet kind of hard.

One year, in one place, it also made a great mess of things.

All the kids had come in for this year's Christmas play. Each brought their own garb and props and left them after the last dry run. Mary had Dad's blue shirt and Grandma's knit shawl. Joseph and the Shepherds came in plaid bath robes from their uncles and tea towels from their aunts. Each angel came with a tin-foil halo and den-floor wings that moms and dads had helped make. The kings came with gifts and laughs and lots of shhhs. In all the rush, I didn't think about gems on crowns and gilt on robes but just had to let it go.

Then came the final night. Amid the joy and noise and bales of real hay for seats and stools and some to fill the angel-choir lofts and the trough, I didn't see that the kings were not there until it was time to start. We tried to find them to give them their crowns and robes — and gifts to take to the Christ child. I wasn't too scared until the choir sang, "Peace on earth, good will to all men."

Then with the sound of a great gust of wind; Leroy, Billy Bob, and Chuck came in through the door. In a big mess, they bumped each other and tripped up the aisle and made lots of noise. They also beamed as they huffed and puffed up to the creche. In their arms were high boots, bright yellow oil-skin coats and, of all things, red fire hats with big yellow threes on them that caught the shine from all 'round the room.

"We got 'em!" the first one said.

"All the things the kings wore!" added the second.

"We had to wait for the fire truck to come back!" said the third.

"I know we're late!" they all said at once.

Like their boy-sized legs, their words were all in twists.

I stood with my mouth wide open as the three began to put small-boy feet in man-sized boots and tried to find small-boy hands in man-sized sleeves to carry the gifts I stood and held for them. The angel choir tried to start over, their words all in a twist, too.

When I found my voice, I said, ""But where are your robes and crowns? Kings wear robes and crowns."

The boys stopped and looked up at me, their warm hearts on the brink of a great cliff. I was about to crush their faith in the tales of the Christ Child born this night (or at least in what grown-ups say).

Then Chuck said. "But Miz D, you said they come from a fah-er!"

From then on, I found a need to use two ears and one mouth, and to be clear in what I chose to tell a child, 'cause kids don't hear what we mean but sure do hear what we say.

That night, I learned from the boys' fright-filled looks a new way to live for Christ — that I should come to him, not in a king's crown and robe, but in ways that share the truths of my life, of who I am. No fear, no fright, none of that — just being and doing the best I can with what I think I heard. Like the kings, my heart needs to come from afar all in a rush and a twist on Christmas Eve. I can hear the tales of kings in crowns and robes or Fire Department clothes — or even rags — as long as I, too, kneel by the Christ Child and give my whole self once more to the true king.

2

THE PLANE TRIPS
FROM HADES

Reba Rhyne

I t kicked off when my brother asked me to join him on a tour
of France. "Man," I said, "Sure. When?" He sent me the info,
and I paid for the trip.

After having been wed for twenty-five years, my bond with my
husband was gone, and I was flying solo. I was so low, it would
have taken a crane to pick me up. I might have been down, but I
wasn't out. I thought that a trip must just be the right pick-me-
up to ease my mind.

Now for *the rest of the story* . . .

My sister-in-law took me to McGhee Tyson Airport in Knoxville
at 9:00 a.m. I was going to JFK, New York City. "Cancelled" was
the word on the sign.

"Come back in two hours," the agent said. "You'll fly into La
Guardia and take a taxi to JFK. You'll have lots of time to make
your 5:30 p.m. flight."

After a fast bite at Wendy's, we tried again. This time I got
on a flight bound for Charlotte-Douglas Airport. At forty-five, I
was on the plane and had taken off on my first-ever flight. Nose
glued to the pane, I loved the scene below — hills, lakes, and flat
land like tiny icons of the real thing on *terra firma*. At Charlotte-
Douglas, the wind blew hard, moving the plane from side-to-
side. I held on to my seat.

"A bit rough," said my seat-mate. We hit the air strip hard and
came to a halt. At the gate, I got off.

After an hour's wait, I was in my seat for the flight to New York City — but, as it turned out, not yet. The crew said they had need of two seats for some kids on their way home. It took most of an hour to get them on the plane.

And then, we were on the strip, going at a fast pace down the lane.

And then — we slid to a halt. What now? "A light on the dash," the pilot said. "We will try to fix the snag from here. It isn't safe to take off with this light on."

No dice!

Back to the gate, and one more hour to fix this cause for delay in my trip. At last, were in the air, and New York City was in sight.

At La Guardia, I picked up my bags, ran for the taxi, and we made a mad dash thru Queensborough for JFK Airport. At the Pan American desk, I found out that my plane had let the gate on the way to Paris, France, but I sure wasn't.

What to do? "Can I get on the one to Paris tomorrow?"

"'Don't know," the man said, "but go to Piedmont Airlines and ask for a meal and a room for the night, and we'll see." Okay. That seemed wise. I had a game plan in mind.

At Piedmont Airlines, they were not in the mood to help. Techs were taking care of old gear with new being fixed in its place. Piedmont Airlines was now US Airways. A kind man, the last part of Piedmont, did give me a pass for a meal and a room at the Holiday Inn.

I left my bags at the JFK bag check and took the bus to my room. A lady from a crew of Delta Airlines rode with me. I tried to get her to chat.

After small talk, she asked, "Have you been at this hotel before?"

"No," I said. "Why?"

"If you hear a tap on your door in the night, don't open the door!"

Ooh! Could I rely on my ears?

With my room key, kit for my teeth, and food from the Inn's

bar, I went to my room, shut the door, and slid the dead bolt.

At three o'clock I heard a rap on the door. It hadn't woken me up, though, for I had never gone to sleep in the first place. I sat up on the edge of the bed and kept as quiet as a church mouse. I heard and felt the beat of my heart. I'd had all I could take and was about to snap. *Is this just a bad dream? Then wake up, Reba Carolyn!*

At ten o'clock the next day, I was again at JFK. I sat down to wait for Pan Am to open at noon.

'time to call home. My father was sick with fear. He'd called any he felt could help. His heart was much eased to hear from me. He said my brother had left a plan for me if I went on to Paris. I took my pen out to jot down the info.

"Are you going to go?" my father asked.

"Yes. I'm here at JFK. When Pan Am opens the door, I'll see if I can get a new ticket."

"Let me know, will you?"

"Yes, I will."

At noon, Pan Am opened the door, but no one was there. Every agent had left on strike. A man came to the door and said, "We'd heard this might happen. Just wait. We have other ticket agents to step in."

In front of a new agent, I told her about the mess I was in, and that I had missed my flight. "I need a new ticket," was my plea.

New on the job, she didn't know what to do. Her boss came over, and I told him about the jam I was in. He put me on the next flight, and I called to let my father know that all was well.

At six o'clock, I was on my way to Paris, France. I asked a teen who sat not far from me, to let me go along as she went through customs. She said okay.

At Charles De Gaulle Airport, I went with her to pick up my bags. They were late off the plane. I got my bags and looked far and wide but couldn't find the girl. So I just went the same way that many of the ones from my flight were going.

I soon stood on the path out of the airport. A man who wore a polo shirt with all the big cities in America on it was in the lane. It was my hope he knew English. I asked about a taxi. He did not know English.

"Taxi?" he asked.

"Oui!"

He aimed a hand, and I took my spot in line.

"Bonjour," I said. *"L'Hotel Mont Parnasse."*

My taxi driver took one look at me and said, "Closed." *If only he knew the mess I'm in!* I thought. Then he let out a big hee-haw and put my bags in the back.

We were pals by the time I got to my hotel. I went to the desk and gave my name.

"No room," the young man said. He claimed to have searched every log.

A light bulb went on. "Are you with a tour?"

"Oui," I said.

"Just go that way," the man said and held his hand to show me the turn to make.

"Merci!"

Soon, I went into a room on an upper floor. I was sure it wasn't my brother's room, but the bags had tags from the area he lived in. This was his tour, and I would find him.

Worn out from no sleep in the last two days, I took a nap on one of the beds. The phone woke me up. "Grab a taxi and come to the *Musée d'Orsay,*" he said.

I did as told. Never have I been so glad to see any human on this earth. I did enjoy the rest of the trip and above all the very, very dull ride home.

3

IN THE DEEP WOODS

Karen O. Allen

The woods, along with the cool, spring nip in the air seemed to call my name and hint it was time for a hike. The crisp smell of pine trees and the crunch of oak leaves under my feet would be a chance to clear my head from the fog of work that had plagued me for the past few months.

I had heard about a trail in the back hills of Leeds, Alabama, not far from where I lived. The trail was deep in the woods with cliffs, huge rocks, and views that would take your breath away. I phoned my friend Pam:

"How would you like to join me for a half-day hike?"

"I like the sound of that," she said. "When do you want to go?"

"Let's go next week. I'll bring O'Malley, too," I said. "He'll love it."

My dog O'Malley went on hikes with me all the time. He was strong and stout with big feet that could scale the rocks. It would be fun for all three of us.

The day soon came. I picked up Pam with dog in tow, and off we went. When we got there, we saw no other cars in the small dirt lot near the trail. To us, two girls and a dog on a lone trail in the woods with no one in sight seemed to beg my question: "Hey Pam, did you bring your gun with you?"

"Yep, I got it," Pam said as she tapped her pack. She didn't make a big deal about it but I knew that she brought it on most of our hikes. She used it once on a big snake. My stance is that you can't do too much to be safe out in the woods.

Our breath turned to smoke in the chill of the air, but the sun felt warm on our faces as it peeked through the clouds. We laced our boots, checked our gear, and hit the trail. We talked for a while, but at mile three our talk ceased. O'Malley still ran back and forth in front of us as if to show us the way. Each mile took us to new heights with each view more grand than the last.

We hiked for about four miles when O'Malley stopped, sniffed the air, and took off down a hill. He liked to go on side-hikes, but this was out of the norm since he did not come back. I called and called, but he still didn't come.

"I'm not sure where that dog is or why he has not come back but I think we best go look for him," I groaned. Pam agreed. We walked back and marked our exit at the place where O'Malley had left the trail. After the noise of leaves ahead, we heard a shrill bark.

"O'Malley, come here," I called.

Not far away we could see him with his head, legs, and feet deep in the ground. He had dug a hole and was in full "hunt mode." I was glad to find him but was mad that he didn't come when I called — until I saw why.

"Pam, get over here," I said. "Now." She rushed over and looked down at my feet.

"Oh my gosh," she said. "Is that a . . . "

She bent down. Under a thin layer of leaves right next to my foot was a toe! It looked to be human. Yes, it was. A human big toe from a white male. It had black hair on it and a thick gross nail. Dried blood was at the base from where it had been sliced clean off the foot. It didn't look that old.

The only words that would come out of my mouth were: "Oh man, this is bad. Real bad."

I jerked O'Malley from the hole just a few feet away. My gut filled with dread as I leaned over to peer into the hole. He, too, had found a human part but his was worse. His looked to be the top of a human head! Hair mixed with dirt and leaves caused me to gasp and jump back.

"Let's get out of here," I yelled. "O'Malley has dug up a head."

Pam reached in her pack and pulled out her gun. My heart raced as I leashed O'Malley and we ran up the hill toward the trail. Only the sound of leaves and soft grunts could be heard for the next four miles as we half-jogged, half-walked back to the car. We were out of breath as I cranked the car and drove straight to the cops in Leeds. Pam phoned ahead to tell them about our grim find.

When we got there, the Chief was at the door. He asked our names and took notes. A half-hour later, tired but pumped from angst, Pam and I led a team back to the trail. O'Malley stayed by my side, as he could sense my fear. We trekked through the woods, up the rocks, and down the hill to the place where we had marked our exit off the trail. We turned right and soon spied the spot where O'Malley had dug the hole. As we drew close, I looked for the toe. We had left it on the ground.

"Where is it? It has to be here." I was miffed.

The team, Pam, and I scanned the area but could not find the toe.

The Chief walked toward the hole. He looked in, then glanced my way. I ran over and looked in as well. I felt sick and fell to my knees as I clawed the ground.

"Where's the head? It was right here. I don't get it. I saw it. I'm sure of it. Well, I guess I'm sure of it. I didn't dig it up. I didn't even show Pam since we got the heck out of dodge and came straight to you. I thought you should be the one to dig up a head, not me! But I don't guess you can do that if there's not one here, huh?"

My thoughts were blurred and dazed as I stood up. The team of cops looked a bit worn and out of sorts, too.

"Some brute has been here since we've been gone and dug this head up. They took the toe, too. Who knows what else they took?"

I gulped and threw my hand to my mouth.

"Oh no! They must have seen us," I said as I grabbed the arm of the cop next to me.

He rolled his eyes. I could feel my face turn red as I tried to hold my tongue. But it was no use.

"Do you think I made this up, Sir? Do you? Come on now. Why would I do that?" I turned toward the Chief: "It's the truth, Chief. I saw a head and a toe just hours ago in these woods. Pam saw the toe, too, didn't you, Pam?"

"Yes, I did. I got a close look. We didn't dare touch it so we could show you right where it was."

"Too bad you didn't," said the Chief. "It would have been good if you had brought it with you. Then we would have some kind of proof of foul play out here. Right now all we can do is search for clues."

The search went on for two days, but no clues were found. Not one. There was no case. How could there be since there was no head or toe? Only a hole my dog had dug.

I don't know what the cops thought of us that day, and I don't care to ask. All I can say is that Pam and I know what we saw on our hike. I guess the truth will die in those woods — along with a chopped-up body with no name.

4

TREASON OF THE HEART

Paul Aaron Hinton

Joshua Karin grew up in rural North Carolina. His family farm was hilly, so the sun set early there. As a boy, Joshua never seemed to care much about time or pain. He could walk for hours barefoot on the steep and rocky trail near his home. Among prickly pears and stink weed, Joshua Karin was at home. His heart was alive in his neck of the woods. But in this story, Joshua Karin is no more a boy.

At eighteen, he took up arms against the Nazis in the great World War. He was made for the Army and soon found that his call was to lead men. What's more, he was the best shot in his entire squad. Joshua could shoot out the eyes of a snake at two hundred yards with no scope to speak of. It was not long before Central Command sent him to join the most elite team of snipers that the U.S. Army had ever seen.

At first Joshua did not feel that he could match up to such men — all made of iron with hearts of stone — when he was just a farm boy from the hills of North Carolina. But as time passed, Joshua came to know that every man in his squad had a life story just like his. They had grown up in the country. They had all put meat on the table; they had all made their way among the thorns.

In due course, Joshua learned that a true sniper is slow in every way he moves. His Commander never let up on this truth. He drummed into his elite team that any step, any sway of the arm, any cough could get them all killed. It didn't take long for Joshua to learn how to sneak as close as ten feet from an enemy and not be seen.

And so, Joshua's true life began with a long ocean to cross. Joshua and his team sat in the belly of a Tramp Steamer and hoped they would be the ones to kill Hitler. To stay sharp, every night, they crawled from bunk to bunk to leave notes in the seams of the Regular Army boys' bunks — notes that always left those "green horns" very upset. During the day, the Sniper Squad were the only ones to go top side. From the crow's nest or the perch on the bow, they fired their sniper rifles at bright pink buoys tossed out by ships at the front of the convoy and kept their eyes out for U-Boats.

After only a week in England, Joshua's squad was split in two units of eight and he was glad to learn that his best bud, Steve, and his Commander were in his squad. They were told that they would drop on the other side of enemy lines and then wait. A big plan was soon to come into play, but no one in Central Command would talk about it. Only one hitch to their part of the plan lay ahead; no one in Sniper School had taught them how to jump from a plane. A quick class on the air strip on their last full day in England was all they were to have.

On the night they took off, the sky was aglow with stars. Joshua saw it as a sign that all would go well. *Or at the least* — he thought, as he took his seat in the C-47 Skytrain — *I hope the stars will not lead us to our doom.*

The trip over the English Channel was far too short but went well. No one had seen them. Not one shot had cut open the thin metal skin of their plane. That had been his deep fear, that he could have died and not ever fired a shot.

First a red light began to flash. It was the sign that they were near the drop point. He stood, his knees weak from fear. Being in a gun fight did not scare him but the thought of a short fall from the sky had him tied up in knots. Then the green light began to flash, and Joshua knew that from this point on, he could never look back. All of his life had been but a game. Now it was it was all too real. Every sway of his arm, every step, every cough could be his last. One, two, three, four, five, six, seven and out he went into the dark night — the last of eight.

He could see the stars once again, and they gave him hope that he might make it. Then a great pop and snap took him back to his true state of fear. His life hung by tiny strips of silk in a tight weave, each inch of it in a strain that he could not begin to grasp. He looked side to side but could not see any of his team. *It's just too dark,* he told his heart; he would see them on the field. The earth below seemed to rise up to meet him. Joshua took hold of the pilot straps and tried to steer, but he knew they wouldn't do much good. His fate was up to luck and the wind.

Then, the earth was upon him. Joshua hit, bent his knees and spun to a stop. His chute fell about him, and Joshua's worst fear was over. He was whole and with his rifle by his side. He began to pack up and bury his chute to cover up any sign that he or his team had been there.

Joshua gazed all about for his team but saw no one. Then he heard an odd-but-human sound. It came from a large oak lit up by the moon. High, near its trunk, what had to be a man was in a slow spin. Joshua's heart sank as he raced to the tree. Once near, he could see that it was his Commander, and the silk lines Joshua had come to trust were bound about his Commander's neck. He was near death, and all Joshua could do was watch as he took his last breath. That very Commander would have given him hell if he had dared to say a word. Joshua fell to his knees and looked up again to see yet one more body in the limbs. This one did not move — no sound, no groans. He could not tell which of his team it might be. And then a warm drop fell on his face.

Josh jumped back. Where were the rest of his team? He dare not turn on his light. He began to run north until he came upon a lake so full of the light of each pin-point of star above that had an echo in the calm water. He then saw three spots in the lake with no stars. Josh gazed hard into the night, and then it came to him. The dark spots were parachutes floating in the water. Not even a swirl came from them. He ran as hard as he could until he came upon a stump near the edge of the lake. He then saw a chute near the stump. His heart raced as he made the last few feet. The "stump" was a set of legs and Army boots stuck in the mud.

Joshua sat down. The night was a lie. The stars were a lie. All but one of his squad was dead and he had no hope that he might find that one alive. He wasn't even sure who was dead. Then it hit him that his Commander would want him to form a plan and move on that plan with the nerve of a snake.

Joshua dug for over an hour to free the man trapped in mud. As his torso came out, Joshua grieved but also thanked God that it was not Steve, his best bud. It was Ted, the only one on the team from the West Coast. Joshua then took Ted as deep in the lake as he could and sank him with a hefty rock from the shore. All he could do about the three team members deep in the lake was hope that their chutes would slip below the water line. He then made his way to his Commander and the man above him. It took him two hours to free them both from the tree. It took one more hour to free the chutes. He towed both of their bodies to the lake and sank them with Ted.

With the sun coming up over the rim of the earth, Joshua took stock of his gear and all he had found on the two in the tree. He had no time to seek a safe place to hide. He lay on a felled tree near the lake and hid his torso with a few broke limbs. He took his rifle and gazed at the world about him. He was in a clear field next to a lake with no homes in sight. So far, luck had been on his side.

Joshua began to slip off into a sleep he could not stop, but then he heard what he had hoped not to hear, the sound of a truck. With rifle in hand, he gazed across the lake and saw his friend Steve in a full run from the woods' edge. He was being chased by a Nazi-marked truck. Joshua took aim on the one who drove and fired. When he missed, the truck sped up to hit Steve from the back. Joshua gaped on as he heard both of Steve's legs snap under the tires. Steve was still alive, but Joshua knew it would not be for long. Joshua took aim as two men came out of the truck with knives drawn. He fired and the men froze in their tracks as the head of their prey blew apart in front of them. Joshua then fired again, and both men fell to the ground as the one shot cut both in two.

Joshua hated God that day. He hated God as he sank his best mate in the lake with the rest of his team. He hated God as he slid the naked torso of each of the two SS men into the lake with Steve. He hated God as he put on the SS uniform that fit him best and drove into a town he had never heard of. He hated God as he climbed the church bell tower and waited for the big thing that was to come. As he heard the heavy American planes fly above, each with a load of bombs, he hated God for giving him a gift that no one should want. He hated God as he saw more chutes land in the fields from which he had come. His heart full of treason, Joshua did what he was taught to do well — what he now hated to do. And when Joshua was over the rage, and the sun began to set early upon the hills of his heart, 223 of Hitler's best lay dead upon the streets of Rouge Du Paradisa.

5

THE MYSTERIOUS MAN

Jewell Utt

On a cold night in November, I drove from New Jersey to Illinois. My eyes, worn from miles of road, begged for rest. Every time my head would fall down, I'd jerk it back up. The lines in the road didn't help since they only served to lull me to sleep. Just as I fought to stay alert, my car hit black ice. I might have dodged it, if I weren't so tired, but I lost the fight. My car slid off the road and ran up the side of a tree. It flipped over two or three times. My head hit the wheel hard, and my world went black. It felt good to give in to sleep.

I woke to a shock: an arm that shook and shook me and a deep voice that yelled, "Wake up, you're not safe. Your car could catch fire. Get up. Get out."

My eyes were wide open now, but my head was fuzzy. "Fire?" I could try and climb out, but the door was stuck and would not give way. Glass was all over the place, and I knew I was hurt. I could taste blood and saw it drip from my head. A sharp pain came from both my arm and a leg. I didn't have the strength to get out, but the strong man was there to help. He pulled me out of the car and dragged me away from it.

"In case a fire might start." he said.

My head spun. I didn't know what to do, and my car was a total mess. Route 80 West had no phone along the way, and I could see no cars for miles. But just then a big Mac truck came into view. The one who drove it pulled over and ran to me. I tried to fill him in on what I knew as he called 9-1-1. Along with tears and gasps, the story spilled out. I turned to ask the first man to fill in the part that I didn't know, but he was gone.

Where did he go? Where had he come from? I could see no house or other car. I looked up and down the road but saw no trace of him. The guy from the truck said he never saw a man with me. The chill in the air did not come close to the chill that ran up my spine. I knew I could not have made it out of the car on my own, and he agreed. He searched about but could not see him. The man was no place to be found.

The haze that hung in the air made the night feel worse. Then a small fire turned into a big one as the car blew up. The man who had helped me was right. I thanked him, though he was not there, and I thanked God. The guy in the truck gave me a sheet to keep warm and stayed with me until help came. When they did, they took me to the E.R.

Five or six days had passed, when the man from the truck strolled into my room. He asked how I was, and I said fine — thanks to him. "The hospital staff has taken good care of me." I had a gash on my head and an arm and leg had snapped. "But *you* don't look so good," I said.

He just stood there and stared at me for a while. Then he spoke.

"That night, at first I didn't see you. All I saw was a light flash on and off, on and off. It looked like a call for help, so I pulled over. That's when I spied your car in the ditch and you on the side of the road. I don't know how you got out of the car on your own. But then you spoke about a man who helped you." He paused. "I don't know where you stand on all this, but I think it was a God thing," he said.

"Yeah, I've had the same thoughts," I said. "Where did the man go who pulled me from the car? Then it hit me: What would have happened to me if you had thought that I already had all the help I needed? You might not have stopped. And you're the one who phoned 911 and stayed with me."

Then he said, "That's just why I think God is in this. If I had not stopped, I might have been killed."

"What?" I was all ears now.

He said it was true. At the same time that he was helping me, the Quick Mart where he had been going was being robbed. Things got out of hand fast, and the men with guns shot up the joint. Every one who had been in the store was killed. By the time I got there, after I saw them put you into the medic van, the place was filled with squad cars. But I was spared from it all. To me, that had to be God."

The truth of his words hit me. I was in awe, for I also could see God's hand in this. Then I shared with him about my deep and long-time faith. Prior to this, he hadn't thought about faith or God. But after this, he had come to know, deep down, that it was true — that God saves and that He saved him that day.

"By the way, what's your name?" I asked.

"Charlie."

I gained a friend that day, but I call him Mac. We have stayed in touch and have met spouses and children. To God we all give thanks.

6

ONE THING OF NOTE

Joylene M. Bailey

"Ewww! Yuck!" I called out, "When was the last time your clan cleaned under this thing? If they are so hard pressed to make this place fit for the Heritage Society, why aren't they here to help?"

The year was 1985. My new husband, Graham, and I had been asked to clean out the old house on the farm. Just the past week, his Grandma had moved to a care home. She wished to sell the farm, but some of her kin hoped she would change her mind and grant it to the Peace River Heritage Society — though the Heritage Society Board didn't seem to care for the idea.

"Not one thing of note in that old place. Bit of a bore," Mr. Browne, head of the board, had been heard to say.

Some of the clan were upset by that and set their minds to prove him wrong. To that end, Graham and I had been dragged into the fray.

Next to the wall with the gilt-framed print of the farm's 90-year-old hip-roofed barn stood the big bulky beast of a stove. It had screeched over cracked tiles as we heaved it away from the wall. With the red pail full of hot suds in hand, I had squeezed in back of the old stove and turned up my nose.

"Eww!"

I knelt down to sponge water onto the floor.

"Need any help back there?" Graham asked from the other side of the stove. "Hey, what's that?"

He waved toward a dent in the wall. It was not plain to see but for the rusty screws every foot or so.

"I don't know," I mused and stood up to get a good look. As I rose, I leaned on the dent and … CRASH! I fell through the wall onto a dark and dusty floor. In front of my nose I could just make out wood steps that led down into a black hole below.

I sneezed.

"Julie! You okay?" came Graham's voice at my sprawled feet.

"Yeah. Graham, what *is* this?"

"I don't know. I've never seen it, and I don't think Mom and Dad ever knew about strange holes in this old place."

"You mean, you lived here all your life and never knew about this?"

"Uh-uh. But how cool is this? Let's check it out!"

"What? There could be bugs and rats down there."

But by then, Graham had switched on a hand lamp. He gave me one.

"We'll never know 'til we have a look. The steps look solid from here. Come on, this could be fun."

I took one last glance back into the bright room I had spilled from, then trailed him down the steps.

Six steps down, we hit hard-packed earth. A long dim hall of sorts yawned ahead of us. The firm earth walls and roof of the shaft seemed sound. Graham had to crouch to allow his six-foot frame through. Even though I didn't need to, I also crouched, in case any bugs chose to drop out of the dirt above.

The hole went on this way for about 40 feet. All at once, it spread open until we stood in a high arched room about the size of a two-car shop. Light poked through slits in the beams above us. We could just make out two walls built of straight, thick tree limbs. Dug into the dirt floor, they reached as high as Graham's head. They were held fast by what looked like strips of thick hide. These log walls formed three stalls. In each of these stalls were bits of aged horse tack. Reins, ropes, lead shanks, and pails hung from the walls on wood nails bored into the logs. Rough wood troughs bulged from the far wall of each stall. I felt as if I'd gone far back in time.

Hushed, we stood there as our lights swept relic after relic out of the dark.

"What on earth?" breathed Graham. "I can't take this in. I thought they were just myths, but —"

He didn't end his thought.

"What, Graham? What?" I spoke in a hushed voice.

In a low voice, filled with awe, Graham said, "My great granddad came to this land first, in the late 1800's I think. He wasn't made to farm, so the tales go. Gramps was the one who built up the farm after great granddad moved on."

Graham picked up a switch from the dirt floor and leaned it next to a wall.

"But great granddad was good with a horse. The tales were that he was a horse thief! He was taken to court many times. But not one charge could ever be proved."

Graham's voice dropped off as we walked the length of the room and came to a large door at the other end. After a few strong tugs, we cracked the door open, and swung it wide. We both screwed up our eyes at the bright light of the sun that flecked through leaves in the dense trees above us.

As Graham hauled the door shut, I lurched through long grass, piles of old wood, and thick brush. When I turned to watch Graham make his way through the snarl, I gasped.

"Graham, if I had not just come through that door I would never have known that a small barn stood there."

Graham turned to look back.

"Well I'll be. It's built into the hill, back of the house. What a job that must have been!" He grinned. "I think we have a horse thief in the clan. You know what this means, don't you?"

He began to laugh. "We just might have one thing of note in this old place, after all."

I smiled and asked, "Who should we call first, Grandma or Mr. Browne?"

7

THE STORY IN THE STORM

Sara Hague

We kids had heard the twenty-year-old tale of the fierce storm that had touched down on the acres of fields and woods about our new home. Green clouds had churned the sky to form cones that twist and turn, that reach down and suck up all things in their path. A chipped gray boat had been tossed into the boughs of a tree and now rocked back and forth with the wind. The box for hooks, line, and bait was wedged in the next tree. The trunk had grown all around the box. Now part of the tree, it would not be moved.

My two brothers and I, hour upon hour, searched through the woods for all kinds of old finds tossed about by that past gale: bed springs to bounce on, pots for tea and an old tool for toast. A bush with pink blooms pushed up through an old screen door, and grass wound its way over and under cracked plates, cups, and bowls.

We plucked out shards of a life we could only guess at. Whose ripped green cap was that? Whose hands poured tea from this pot? Who burnt their toast in this metal trap door for bread? We could only dream. So many thoughts these finds stirred. Did they all make it through the storm? Were some sadly lost? Who could tell?

Wind the clock about thirty years, a spouse, five kids, and three moves later. From Minnesota to Texas to California to Oregon at last, we found our new home in a land that's green and grows friends into kin.

Two doors down lived a lady who's kind and tough, hard as

nails and soft as chick fuzz. Her smiles beamed grace and good will to my kids as we strolled past, but her eyes said she'd seen too much and felt too much to trust us.

We passed back smiles and waves over the fence day after day, until one night we heard a boom and a crash from her back yard. Power surged, and wires popped and sprayed her trees and house with smoke and sparks. I raced down the walk to pound her front door, to wake them and check, to make sure all were safe in her home.

Her sleep-weary eyes peered out through the screen, and her hands shook to open the door. "We're ok. No fire. The power guys will be here soon," she said and pulled the door wider to let me into her dark home. She struck a match and set out ten small tea lights on her table. Her now calm hands held an old china pot, poured mint tea into small cups, and then showed me a chair to draw close. She stared at the tiny flames and told me her story.

"I grew up on a farm in Minnesota with my two brothers and my mother and father. We kids loved it there, and Mom and Dad were so proud of their farm. When we were done with our chores, my big brother, Bob, loved to catch fish down in the pond with our dog, Fran. My other brother, Jim, and I would run through the woods to try to snag a wild bunny or skip rocks in the creek. Oh those were good days…until…"

Her eyes dipped down to the depths of her cup, and her thumb rubbed the rim with care. For a few breaths I thought the walls might go up again, and I'd be on my way home. But then her eyes turned back to the flames, and she said with a soft, slow voice, "It was a hot day with no breeze, and the air felt so thick and dead that it was hard to breathe. Bob begged Mom to let him go fish on the pond, and Jim and I whined all day to go swim. 'After chores,' was all she would say. Bob went and sulked in the barn while he cleaned out the hens' mess, and Jim and I went out to pull more weeds in the bean patch.

"We were only half done when the sky turned an ugly shade of green and the wind picked up. The clouds curled 'round and we saw a dark swirl of a cone shape dip down toward our tree line. Jim yelled to me to get in the house, that he would grab Fran. Mom ran out toward the field to call Dad. I can still see her wave her arms like a fury, but I never saw Dad. He was up over the hill in the corn field, I guess.

"I slammed the door shut, crouched down, and screamed out through the small glass pane for Bob. The barn was too far away. The wind ripped half the roof clean off the barn, and I couldn't see Mom any more. Bob's boat sailed over the house and past the tree line. Stuff flew all over the place out there. I saw Jim crawl on his belly and grab onto the bush near the old pump. He had our dog under one arm, and his legs flew out and up in the air. That storm tried to pry him right off that bush, but he wouldn't budge. I just cried through the glass over and over, 'Jim! Don't let it take you!' Then it got loud and dark, and the whole house shook and broke apart. I held onto the pipes on the wall and cried and wished it was over. When I let my eyes open again, I only saw Jim and the dog. The rest were gone."

There was a knock at the door. The power guys were there to fix the grid. She wiped her eyes and squeezed my hand. "Thanks for being here to check on us, to make sure, you know…"

"I'm so sorry for your loss. There are no words for that. Thank you for the tea and for your story," I passed her the tea cup. "One day I need to tell you about where I grew up. It has to be part of your story. You won't belie—."

This knock was loud. "Please, come again." Her small smile through her tears shone iron grace and good will as she waved me past the work crew on her porch. She turned back toward her house, but then her steps paused, "How about after the kids head to school?"

"See you at 9:00," I dipped my head in thanks.

8

FEAR

Toni Armstrong Sample

Pennsylvania was a blur as Dave and I began our east-coast quest. With the Fedor book to guide us and our R.V. well-stocked, we had ten days to search for new sights. A seven-hour drive from one end of our home state to the other found us at our first stop. In Philadelphia we found great food, a cracked Liberty Bell, and a fun day in the place that bears the name, "City of Brotherly Love."

A sound sleep brought us to day two, as we headed to Norfolk, Virginia. Day three we were on Pawley's Island, Georgia. With the book of trails and tales still in hand, we crossed the Florida state line on day four.

The town of St. Augustine claims to be the old lady of the south. She lies a short jaunt south of Jacksonville. The streets are tight, more suited for a horse and cart or a hike by foot, than for a car. The city's old charm drew us in. Dave and I spent the day, ready to snap many shots, as we did a slow stroll from site to site.

With a warm invite from the VFW, we dined that night on fresh Florida food from the sea and slept in our van. Curled up on our queen bed, under a cozy down quilt, we woke with the rise of the bright sun.

Today we would find the Fort and walk through a saga of the past.

My first sight of the Fort's vast walls of grey and white stone took my breath away. The hair on the back of my neck rose as a chill ran through me. When I looked back on that day, I thought, *Why didn't I heed those signs?*

Dave was like a child. He couldn't wait to check out the Fort and hear the tales of the flint-end shafts and field-gun blasts that had shot chunks of rock from the huge stones. For more than three hundred years the Spaniards, Indians, and English had fought each other on this land. The rocks that were used to build the fort walls could thwart the crash of a foe's fire. Forts built of hard rock, under the same fire, were ripped apart. "Coquina is not only soft; it is a lightweight building material," said our guide "so that many of the fort's walls had to be made six-to-ten feet thick."

As Dave and I trekked about the Fort, we found a shaft, only about four feet high, of the soft rock that led to the spire. With Dave to my rear, we began to walk bent-legged through the long shaft. As I stepped out onto the dirt floor of the tower-room, a strong force hit me with a power so great that it caused my body to bend at the waist.

With a clutch at my chest, I fled full tilt back to the light. In alarm, Dave came after me. He grabbed my arm in the Fort Square, swung me against his chest, and hugged me tight to him until I was calm.

"What was that?" he asked.

"I don't know. I felt like a ton of weight had hit me square in my chest. I need to leave — now!"

From that day on, I have lived with the fear of being trapped. I have to sit in aisle seats in shows and at church. I have fled from any chance of an MRI. Prior to this time, I would search about in caves with no alarm — even ones where I would have to hike miles under the earth. Now, the fear of that day walks with me.

On that same trip, we went to the Gulf Coast, and in Mobile I tried to tour a U.S. sub. I was not able to go below. Docked next to the sub was the USS Alabama Battleship. After going only one deck down on the large ship, I had to leave the tour.

Years passed, and one day Dave called me to come to our TV room.

"Listen to this, Hon," he began. "National Geographic is doing a piece on Fort Augustine. They have all these well-equipped experts and the stories of many who have gone through events like yours. They have the skill, time, and aid to search for the cause."

With shaky legs, I sat down to listen. In this show, facts were made known about the tower, where the fear had flowed through me. Many years ago, a woman and her lover had been placed in that turret by her officer husband — to starve and die. Indians had also been jailed in the dark space to face the same fate. Claw marks on the walls had shown that the Indians had used each other to climb upon in an attempt to scale the walls and live.

Do I believe in Spirits? How can I not? I believe in the Holy Spirit.

I am sure that what I felt though new to me was very real. Had I been touched by those long dead who have not found peace or been able to move past the place of their deaths? Was it their angst that I felt? I don't know.

It seems that I was very open to such events, at least in the deep south. A short time later, I was touched once again, much in the same way as with the first. This time, when I felt that same fear, I was in a type of alley that was all under the ground — a part of the Underground Railroad in Charleston, South Carolina.

Do I want this eerie touch to occur again? No. I pray every day for all the souls of the dead who are yet to find peace.

The Holy Spirit, who lives in me, is the only such type of being that I need, and the only one I want. With the Holy Spirit I have no fear.

9

JUST MY LUCK

Laura Luptowski Seeley

Even though my dad was lucky, that gene was not passed down to me so I don't often take risks with my money. Still, a few years ago, I took a chance on the Michigan Lottery's Daily 3 and Daily 4 games.

When I walked into the store, I had to ask the store clerk how to fill out the game slips. "Do I choose 50¢ a play, or $1? What does it mean — boxed or straight? Do I play once or twice a day? How much could I win?" I began to fill in the tiny dots on the form. Twice, I had to tear it up and start over. In the end, I just looked up and said to the clerk, "These are my picks. Why don't you just fill this in for me?" By the time I was done, the line in back of me was out the door.

I came up with a plan. For just one week, I'd play 271, 3105, and 5080 twice daily, for the 12:59 p.m. and the 7:29 p.m. draws, $1 each. I could afford $6 a day for a week. I played them straight — which I had learned meant I could win up to $500 if 271 came in, and up to $5,000 if 3105 or 5080 came in. Each day, I'd check to see if I'd won. By the fourth day, I thought: *This is not worth it. I should not waste my time and money.*

Then it was Day Five — April 13. Since I felt that 13 was lucky for me, I chose to try again. Early in the day, I pulled up to the store and placed my wager for the 12:59 draw.

I'd planned to stop at the store at the end of the day to play my picks just prior to the 7:29 draw. But on my way home, due to chest pains, I went to the ER. By the time I left there, it was too late to place my wager.

Late that night, back at my house, I checked to see what had come in on the 7:29 draw. Of course! "271." Total paid out: $500.

"No, no, no!" I cried as I ran down the stairs to tell my husband about my bad luck. Once I calmed down, I was able to laugh it off. Kind of.

Early the next day — Day Six — as I was on my way out the door, I saw a bright flash of light in my eye. I knew this could be the sign of a major eye issue, so I went to have it checked out. After a brief exam, I was given a clean bill of eye health. I got back in my car and went to my event. In my haste, I drove right past the party store and did not stop to place my wager for the early game.

That night, by the time I was on my way home, it was past the 7:29 draw time. So again, I did not get a chance to buy my picks. *Oh well,* I thought. *At least I saved six bucks today!*

When I got home, I sat down at my desk, turned on my Mac, and pulled up the Michigan Lottery site. There on the screen I saw it: "5080." Total paid out: $5,000. Just my luck! I put my head down on my desk and cried.

"What are the odds?" a friend asked the next day. Yes, what *are* the odds?

I haven't played since.

10

Patty and Me

Lin Daniels

Every kid has that buddy, that one-of-a-kind friend who walks with them as a child, right? Think back, I'm sure you must have had one? Or maybe even more than one?

My buddy was a girl my exact age, with straight brown hair and brown eyes, just like me! When I saw a photo of me, it was just like the one that my mind held of her. Even her teeth and smile were a match for mine. In fact, one day I lost a tooth, and the very next day she lost the same tooth but on the other side of her mouth! How odd was that?

My buddy and I liked to play the same games and could play alone for hours. No need for any other kids — the two of us were okay alone. We loved any sports with a ball, and any other thing we could build. Often, we would act out scenes, like a dance star with her best moves or a TV hero who saved the world or some other full-of-drama event.

It was not usual for me to do bad, wrong things. But if I did, my Mother put me on the stool. And wasn't that my buddy on the other stool? Mom said I had to be still and could not talk out loud. Not able to move and being quiet was like being in jail. Later my buddy made a quip that she hated it as much as I did.

At night, my buddy slept in the same room. If I was full of fear, she would hop into bed with me. As I look back, I can just about feel her body — cozy, right next to mine — and the warm touch of her hand as she held mine. And all my fears left.

I could tell my buddy about any, and every, part of my life. But most of the time I didn't. No need to since I felt that at any given time, she was aware of all my thoughts. A part deep in me felt as if I were "one" with my buddy, since we were so close.

My parents knew that my buddy and I were a pair, that she was with me in just about every area of my days and nights. In fact, they gave her a name, Patty. Why did they choose that name? I would have voted for a name that was not so usual, one more off the wall. But the name Patty stuck. It seems that was one of the girl names my parents most liked. When Mom would yell time to eat, she would call my name. And if I didn't come right away, she would add "Patty!"

Through all my days of being a child, Patty and I were the best of friends. Even now, as an adult, if she is not near, I miss her. So is she real, with flesh and blood? Or just a part of the drama skit I liked to play?

11

GOD WILL LEAD

Steve Duke

The three boys had been friends since ninth grade. They lived on the same street. Now in twelfth grade and too smart for their own good, they had talked their moms into a trip up the Perdido River — just the boys.

At first, things were great. They had run that old motor boat the ten miles up to a high place on the banks. There, while Bill and Steve set up the camp, Jack took the boat for a ride. But the ride was too long so the boat ran out of gas. Quiet now, the boat slid back into the bank at the camp.

'no use to start a fuss now. What was done, was done.

Jack stuffed some paper in a hole in a tree and set fire to it. Who knew why? Ants swarmed out of the tree and onto all the gear. It was too late to search for a place to move the camp. So, the boys put all the gear back in the boat and cast off. It was a poor start. They had but one oar, and it was pitch black on the river. Jack went to the front, curled up, and went to sleep. Steve and Bill took turns on their feet, using the oar first on one side and then the other to keep the boat away from the banks. The half moon helped some but not much. Dark is dark, and these three teens were scared.

At least five times, the river forked. Each time, the boys paused with the oar and tried to make up their minds which fork to take. And each time, one fork would be dark and the other would have scores of fire flies, with their lights going on and off, on and off.

Steve said, "You're going to think I'm nuts, but I think that is a sign from God to take the fork with the lights." Bill did not say a word. He just gave a nod of his head. Four more forks in the river and it was the same — dark on one fork and lights from the bugs on the other. Each time, Steve said the same thing, "God leads us home."

It made no sense — same swamp, same air, and same trees. But Steve knew what the other two did not: God does not have to make sense. He can do what He wants, when He wants. On this dark night, He was using bugs to show the boys the way home.

The boys got to the fish camp at 1:00 A.M. Bill used a dime to call his mom to come get them.

All three were in church Sunday.

12

MOM'S NEW PET

Heidi Gaul

The lion perishes for lack of prey, and the cubs of the lioness are scattered.

Job 4:11

I heard the shot and its echo from out back, by the side of the barn where the woods get thick. We lived way out from town on a dirt road that turned to mud when it rained. There were a lot of folks out there, not just my kin, so I had friends to play with after chores. And there was that old one-room school house about a mile down the lane. It was the 1970s, and I was ten.

I ran to find Dad, to see what he'd bagged. If it was deer we'd have meat for a long time.

"Got her!" He yelled. "We won't need to worry over the hens so much, now that's she's gone. I knew I could beat her at her game."

It wasn't a buck or a doe or even a fawn.

Dad laughed. "That wild cat stole a dozen of our fowl during the past few months."

He was right, but I didn't like what he'd done. She was too pretty to die.

As I looked down at the big cat, her fawn fur now streaked with blood, I felt sad. Her gold eyes were open and stared, as if she were okay. But she wasn't.

I stood by Dad for a long time. Didn't say a word.

Then Mama come out the back door — fast —and the screen slammed shut.

Her hair was up in a bun and a lot of the strands had slipped free and made a kind of halo about her face, as if she were an angel. To me, she sure was.

When she reached Dad and me, she sighed, and knelt down next to the cat. "Pete." Her voice was so quiet as she said my Dad's name.

He walked over to her and set his hand on the top of her back.

She shook a bit. I guess she was sadder than I was. "I know it had to be done," she said, "but look at her. She was a piece of art." Tears spilled down her cheeks like a creek.

That's when the tiny ball of fur came out of hiding and stopped right at the edge of the trees. It was maybe two pounds and looked so brave and sweet all at once.

Dad raised the rifle and took aim, but right then Mom stood up.

"No, Pete. Don't."

"It's the kind thing to do. She'll starve to death."

Mom went as close as she could to the baby wild cat.

It didn't back away but gazed at her, as if to ask, "What's wrong with my mama?"

Mom turned and spoke to Dad, her voice so low I could only just tell what she said. "Let me have her."

Dad shook his head. "That's nuts, woman."

Which it was. But Mom can set her mind to a thing and hang on like a bird on a wire. She meant what she said. "I'm keeping her. That's all there is to it."

Dad let her hug him. He shook his head one more time and then strode to the shed. He called back to us, "If she gets even one of the hens, Rose. Even one."

Mom tsk tsked at him and told me to run and get a bowl of cream for the cat. And to think of a name. The whole time I was in the house and poured the milk, my mind was busy. By the time I got out there, she had the cat in her hands. It mewed like any other cat.

I set the dish on the ground, and she put the cat by it.

She ruffed my hair. "What are going to name her, honey?"

"Yeller." I had seen the film only the week prior and thought it fit. She had that gold and gray fur like her mom's.

"Yeller it is."

Dad dragged the mama's body to hang it over the barbed wire fence. That way, the other folks would know he'd shot the cat so they didn't need to worry about it again.

But he never told them about our new pet.

From the day Yeller moved into my room, life was fun. She loved to play with my socks and a piece of rope my Dad brought in. At night she curled up at the foot of the bed, and I went to sleep with the sound of her purr in my dreams.

While I was at school, Mom took care of her. She sewed clothes for her, which bugged Dad to no end, but they fit her and she looked cute — as if Mom had a baby girl again. She trimmed Yeller's claws and smacked her when she tried to bite.

After a few months, Mom had Yeller trained like a dog and walked her all over our farm on a leash. And she learned some good tricks. She could lie down, play dead — which I hated — sit, and beg. But the best one was hard to grasp. It couldn't be!

The first time I saw her do it, I'd snuck in early from school. I saw Mom in the den with her back to me. She was on her knees in front of Yeller, and Yeller sat there like a big dog.

Mom said, "Four."

Yeller tapped the rug four times.

Mom said, "Good girl," and stuck a piece of bacon in Yeller's mouth.

Yeller licked her jowls, and Mom said "Twelve."

Twelve soft taps on the floor.

I must have gasped. Mom turned and saw me. She wasn't mad as I guessed she would be. "Smart cat, huh?"

That was the start of Yeller's fame. All my friends came to see her do her tricks, and Mom had some of her friends come watch, as well.

We let in only those whom we could trust to keep it quiet. We didn't want her to be taken away or shot. We loved her too much.

Yeller was the best cat I ever had. She lived to be twenty. By then, I had moved away and Dad had passed on. The last time I saw her, she was lying on the porch next to Mom on her cane chair. I walked over and gave Mom a kiss and bent down to pet Yeller.

Her purr was loud as she twitched her bob tail. I said, "I love you, you big cat."

The next morning, she was gone. Just got old and tired, I guess.

One thing I'm sure of. When I get to stand face to face with Jesus, she'll be there, too. And every now and then, she will count out the ways she's been blessed — one by one.

13

FINDING SCOT

Pamela Groupe Groves

The firm voice of Doctor B. rose above the whir and beeps of the ICU tools that worked to keep Scot alive. "Wiggle your finger, Scot," he said. When Scot did not move, my sister's loud voice joined in. In a hushed tone, with my face near his ear, I said, "Scot! Scot, this is your sister Pam. Wiggle your finger." Our voices spread through the ICU as we grew more and more upset. We knew that Doctor B planned to stop all efforts to keep Scot alive if our brother did not move — soon.

Less than a day prior, an ICU nurse had called to say, "Our social worker has been on a search to find Scot's family. This emergency number was found in an old medical-clinic file." After a slight pause, her calm voice added, "We think Scot had been lying on the floor in his room for two or three days before the rooming-house manager found him in a coma. He has been in our ICU for five days in critical condition." After four years, my "baby" brother had at last let us know where he was — 'though it was through scary words from an ICU nurse two states away.

This phone call led us to our brother's side where we tried to get him to show us that he heard our pleas of "Wiggle your finger, Scot!" I began to sense the tiny bit of hope in Doctor B fade. My sister, Tracey, kept up a loop of quiet prayer with every so often a loud, "Wiggle your finger, Scot!" .I couldn't look away from Scot's hand. Then, I froze when my eyes seemed to play a trick on me; I could not speak. Tracey spoke for all of us with a scream, "His finger moved!" Doctor B looked a bit stunned but then, in a calm voice, said, "Ok, we will give him one more day."

14

FALL IN TEXAS

Leah Hinton

The sun was still low in the pale blue sky. Grey clouds sat like war chiefs with swirls of pink and gold at their base. I could smell the rain in the air. This didn't shock me. Rain came each day now that it was fall in Texas, one of the best times of the year. In fall, the sun's heat fades and a cool breeze whips the last of the leaves from the trees. When the heat goes away, I can feel sane. As if I can take a breath and not die.

From my school room, I made a trip to my car — the fifth one so far. This time I brought in a box of treats for all the kids in my class. I wrote out the day's plans on the white board at the front of the room. As on each day of this school year, my son came with me so he could hang out with his friends for an hour until class time. That day, the boys walked at the woods' edge on the far side of the school yard.

He and his friends had shared their big plans with me. Their dream was to build a high fort in a big tree, but first they had to find a tree, both tall and strong. The woods were full of small trees with weak limbs that had their growth hurt with the drought from June until then. I knew their search would be long and might not turn up the right kind of tree, but it was their hour to kill, so off they went.

I could hear their calls out in the yard. They laughed. They ran. They did what boys do in that free and easy way of boys. I tried not to envy them their joy and got back to the work at hand. Time stood still as it seems to do when I skip my a.m. java. I was deep in thought when my son ran in. Words fell from his mouth in a heap, and he had to start again.

"Mama, I just saw a girl. She's dead, Mama. Come quick!"

My son tells the truth. But this felt like a tall tale. I thought he let his mind get the best of him in the woods, or maybe his friends had tried to fool him.

I didn't jump up. I didn't move fast. I wrote ten more words on the board.

"Mama!"

"Hold on." Then I saw his face. His skin was white, but his cheeks were red as if he had run the whole way back to me. His breath came in puffs, fast and hard. His bright blue eyes shown dark with fear. *My son tells the truth. He does not lie,* I thought.

"Show me."

He took off like a jet and ran to the far side of the school yard and back. I had gone ten steps to his two laps of the yard.

"Not so fast," I said as I put fire under my feet to make quick work of the last few yards until the tree line.

I stepped up to the edge where the grass meets the road. "Where?"

"There, she's face down in the creek."

From where I stood I saw only woods and mud and leaves. My gaze grew dim as I tried to see what my son swore was there.

"Baby, I don't —"

Then I saw a shoe — a shoe with a foot in it. The foot was at the end of a leg in blue jeans. I ran my eyes up the creek bed and there she was, her face in the water of the creek.

Sad.

Gone.

Dead.

I took my son and held him.

"Mama, we tried to save her, but the creek is too high. I couldn't do it."

"Baby, you are a brave boy. But she is dead. You can't save her."

My son's face didn't look like the face of a nine-year-old boy.

He aged in that brief time since he had begun that walk with his friends. They all did. His eyes did not shine as bright as they had when he woke up that day.

I tapped three keys on my phone, 911, gave my name, and told them where we were and where she was.

In no time, a cop car pulled up. Soon a fire truck came, too.

My son took their words in stride like a brave young man. They called my son a hero. They said that no one had known where the woman was, that now her son could know that his mom is with Jesus. "Good job!" they said.

Even when big things drop on our lives, we still have to live. We still need to feed the dogs, take out the trash, and do all the mom things that we do day in and day out. Work won't let grief own the day. In this case, grief found a way to worm deep into my mind so that it sat hard and still until I felt it in my gut. My thoughts swam about one main source of worry: *How do I save my son from bad dreams? How do I take away the grown-up world that has claimed a place in him now so that he can be small again?*

That night, I went to pick up milk at the Tom Thumb store down the road from our school.

"Hi Andrew. How are you?" I said to the old man with the mind of a child, who bags my milk each week.

"I'm not good, Miss Leah. I got some bad news. Miss Penny had done gone, and she be with Jesus now, uh huh."

"Oh no, Andrew. How?"

"My boss say she got found by a bunch of kids out by the church. Ain't no way to tell the why? Just her time I'm like to say."

Dread swept in my mind. It couldn't be. "That's a sad story you have there, Andrew." I didn't say more to him. No need. The tale is in her life, and now in her death, not in how or where she was found.

The next week, my son and his friends stood at the back of the church. No more than 30 yards from where she was found, and heard her son talk of his mom. We heard her husband speak words of love. Penny was joy and life and love. And all of her gone.

My son shook her son's hand. He shook the hand of her husband. They told him they were so glad that he found her before the first frosts had come. They told him that no one had thought to look in the woods for her.

Back in the car, my son said, "Why did they thank me? I couldn't save her."

"Baby, fear can hurt bad too. Fear, when you can't find the one you love. Your mom. Your wife. But she is with God now, and that takes her son's fear and her husband's fear away. They are still sad. But they thank you, for now they don't feel fear for her. God did good through you."

"Mama, can I pray for her and for her son and her husband?

"You bet, Baby."

"And Mama?"

"Yes, Baby?"

"I don't want a fort."

15

BIRD TAXI ME

Lisa Worthey Smith

What else could I do? The tiny wild bird had hopped onto my hand so I gave him a ride over to a bloom for a sip. He plunged his face into the open petals so his tongue could reach far down into the depths and lick up the sweet gift there. Then he raised his head and used his tongue to wipe his lips, or, in this case his beak, and slurped up all the stray drops. He raised his eyes to look at me and chirped "Come on, let's go to the next one!" *I promise that is what I heard!*

What else could I do? Each time he leaned toward one, I took him close for a visit. He was my GPS as we strolled the area to all the open buds, so he could drink all the sweet drops we could find. At one point, I told him that the heat of the day made me need a break in the shade. His look said, "I agree."

What else could I do? I took him with me to a shady spot under the maple tree and sat in a chair. A breeze found us, and we both turned our faces toward it. As he sat in my palm he began to scratch his head, then used his long beak to scratch his back and his belly. *This dirty bird needs a bath,* I thought.

What else could I do? I set him on a twig while I found an old lid from a tub of sour cream. I filled it with three or four spoons of water and added a small rock in it so he wouldn't slip. He turned his head to the side, leaned over, and used one eye to get a good view. He chirped to me that he liked the idea of a clean pool of his own.

What else could I do? I placed my hand near him and he hopped back in his "seat" for a ride. When I brought him close to the edge of the lid, he dipped his beak in the water and raised it high to let the drop run down to his face. His eyes wide with joy, he hopped onto the rock in his pool. He jumped in and out of the water again and again. It was a one-bird pool party! He splashed and played and chirped with bird glee. I was sure he was clean after all that, but now he was soaked to the bone.

What else could I do? I took him back to a place in the sun where he could hop onto a small twig. He shook out the extra water and used his long beak to preen his back and tummy. His feet reached up to scrub off all the loose dirt from his face and head. In the sun, he sat clean and proud until his eyes closed half shut. I could see that a bird nap time was about to begin.

What else could I do? I took a break from my taxi duty and napped in the shade while he napped in the sun until he was ready to call me for our next trip.

16

OH, TO HAVE SEEN HIM!

Charles Huff

In the 1930s a lot of oil came out of the ground near my home in southern Illinois. My high school chum Gary lived next door to me in the heart of one of the oil fields. Roads coursed past and through farm fields with small lanes that split off to pumps and tanks still in use. In our spare time, Gary and I liked to drive the old roads we had never been on just to see what we had never seen.

Mid-year 1967 gave me an awe-filled day. It began with a light rain that had left a thin sheen and puddles on the pocked road. The sun's rays sliced through gaps in the clouds. Gary and I chose that time to go for a drive in his '55 Mercury — a tank of a car that hugged the road with ease. The rain had cleaned the air, and breaks in the clouds gave way to more blue sky and sun. We talked over the shlush and splat of the tires and the sound of "Brown-eyed Girl" on the radio.

Ahead of us, an oil-field truck pulled out onto the road. A step up in size from a pickup, it carried a tank on its bed. "I hope what's sluicing off that truck is just rain." When we reached the spot where the truck had pulled out, Gary tensed.

"What's wrong?"

"I can't steer the car. It must have been oil and not rain we saw."

"Slow down."

"I'm trying. Where did this curve come from?" Gary fought to slow down and steer as the car hurled toward the ditch on his side of the road. But the car seemed to pick up speed. The car seemed to pass over most of the ditch with ease, but then the front left tire hit the banked edge. When the front of the car veered up, the ground dropped from sight. The view in front of us was puffy clouds mixed with blue sky — and two straight tree trunks. Each trunk was 6 to 8 inches wide and each in line with a head lamp.

The jolt into the air slammed Gary onto my left side. Built too early for seat belts or air bags, the car was a closed heavy box not made to fly. At some point, both of us left the seat. The car's weight brought us back to earth, and we slowed to a stop. Gary's hip had landed half on and half off my lap, with his foot on the gas, not the brake. The wet grass caused the tires to spin but not catch.

Gary slid back behind the wheel, put his foot on the brake, shifted to park, and turned off the motor.

"Are you okay, Gary?"

"Yes. You?"

"Yeah. At least I think so, but what happened to the trees?" We got out of the car to check for any scrape, gash, or dent from the trees. I circled the car. "What the — ? Gary, the trees were in our way, right?"

Gary looked up from the front of the car. "Yeah, why?"

"If they were in our path, wouldn't they be pushed down in front of the car?" But the trunk of each tree was flat on the ground at a right angle to the car. "Your car is stopped on top of them in the middle."

Gary and I searched for any signs of where the car could have crashed into the trees — each front panel, the head lamps, the grille, the frame, the tires — but we could not find one dent, piece of bark, or any scuff mark. Not a thing to show that the car had hit the trunks. Not even the trees showed signs of a blow. We stood there, stunned.

That's when I thought of Samson when he pushed the columns. "Is this the work of an angel?"

Oh, how we wished we could have seen him!

17

OLD NEWS

Penny Hunt

S he didn't like me. I didn't like her, and we both knew it.

When I caught sight of her near the eggs and milk I thought, "I'll duck down the next isle, act as if I didn't see her, and move on." But a stock boy with a huge load of boxes blocked the way. I was stuck with no way out, and she was headed my way.

She drew near, and I gave her a quick, "Hey Ellen," then looked down at the ice pops on sale in the cold case. "Hey," she replied, and came to a stop right next to me.

My plan was to get as far from her as I could—as fast as I could. I was about to leave the ice pops and head down the bread isle, when what I call the Holy Ghost bell rang in my heart.

"Don't be like that. You don't have to like her. Just love her. Treat her the way you want her to treat you."

No way! I thought. *She's mean as a snake.*

Just talk to her.

I looked at Ellen then, really looked at her for the first time in a long time. She was more than mean. She was scared, and there was no light in her eyes.

What I saw didn't change her sour face or all the mean things she had said and done, but it did change me. It took the fear of her from me and made me bold to ask, "Have you heard the news?"

"What news?" Oh, she was all ears now.

"We have a big storm on its way, and I hear it will be a bad one."

"Are you sure? I haven't heard a word about that."

"Well, that's what they said on the TV last night. It's why I'm at the store right now. I want to be ready."

With a hard look in my cart she said, "So, that's why you have water, cans of food, and boxed milk in there. I thought you were one of those nuts that hoards food for the day the world will end."

Let it go.

"No. No end-of-the-world worry here. I just want to be set if the lights go out and we end up with no water. I'm on my way to the Duracell rack next. How are you set for storm goods?"

"I'll get by."

"Good. I just think it's best to have more than less if need be."

"I guess so."

She made no move to leave. The pause went on for too long. I couldn't think of more to say so I backed up, turned to leave, and said, "Take care and be safe."

She didn't say a word, just stood there and let me go.

Later I watched a bag boy help Ellen load her car with jugs of water and bags of can goods. It felt good to have been nice to her, and she had been sort of nice to me too. *One-step-at-a-time.*

The sky was azure blue as I drove home. It was hard to think a bad storm was on the way, but that's how storms are here in the South. They come and go like hit-and-run cars. Thanks be to God for TV news and Storm Watch.

That night, as I washed up from our meal, the sky was still bright, and the sun was setting pink with not so much as a stiff wind. I closed the door as the gray of dusk brought a chill to the air and thought how much I hate storms at night.

I moved to the den and sat next to my husband to watch the next show we had stored on the DVR. We had been gone for a few weeks. A bit of "News at Eleven" played at the end of the show. It was an ad of sorts for the Peach Blossom Festival that took place the day after we left.

Oh, no," I moaned. "The Storm Watch we saw last night was for weeks ago, wasn't it?"

I had to call Ellen. With a lump in my throat I picked up the phone. One ring. Just three more to go and I could talk to her phone and not face her wrath. Dang! She picked up on two rings. No way out again.

"Ellen? I have to talk to you."

"No," she said. I have to talk to you. I have to tell you how bad I feel. I've been wrong about you from the start. I've been a fool and very much want to make things right with us. Do you think we could meet for lunch?

"Sure, Ellen," I choked. "I mean, I guess so. That would be great, but what I called to tell you is that I was wrong about the storm."

"I thought so. But let's not talk about that. Let's talk about when we can meet. Do you like tea?"

In ways you could never imagine I work things for the best when you trust Me.

18

POPE GREGORY AND THE WAR TRIBE

Tom Kennedy

Pope Gregory was in a sweat. How could he change the ways of a war tribe and tell the chief about Jesus? The tribe had just turned friends with Rome, so they moved from the land of Germany to Roman lands and put down roots. The good news was that the tribe had no more wars to fight. The bad news was that every day the men of the tribe would get drunk and start fights with their friends. Now and then the whole war tribe would brawl with those tribes who lived close by. As a rule, they brawled and fought when they were drunk. And they were drunk a great deal of the time.

The tribe's chief began to fear a new war with Rome, and he knew that the Romans would crush his newly weak tribe. He came to Emperor Lukas to ask for help. Lukas went to Gregory, as pope of Rome, to give him the task to solve this mess. The two men then set up a meet with Gregory, the tribe's chief, and its high priest.

In fact, Emperor Lukas felt that the best way to tame this tribe was for Gregory to make Christians out of them. The high priest was mad when he heard that, some because he was at odds with change but more that it might mean the tribe would have to give up their cult and creeds. Then he would not have a job. Yet both the priest and the chief knew that the clash among the tribe's men and the strife with those who lived close by had to stop. So, they cut a deal. Gregory would send a Christian priest who would help solve the tribe's plight. The pope had some hope, but all three of them also had doubts that it could be done.

After they talked, Gregory thought and prayed for three days. At the end of that time, a young priest on his staff put forth a plan. *It might work*, thought Gregory. He had faith that God had shown him the priest who could change the tribe.

This young priest, named Justin, was well-trained in the Christian faith. What's more, he was bright and well-versed in most of the trades and skills used in Roman lands. Soon after Gregory's priest reached the tribe, he tried out his plan. The high priest of the tribe worked behind the scenes to wreck it. After a month, no change in the tribe could be seen. The priest stepped back and saw that he would have to change his views if he was to help the tribe break with their coarse way of life. He sensed he must first get to know the tribe and learn from them, and then it might be that he could help. Then, by God's grace and power, the tribe would hear him and try his plans. So for the next month he watched and came to know more and more about their way of life and their plight.

What he saw that first month was that some of the tribe were sick. He found that the tribe's waste was soaking into the well. He talked to the chief who asked the tribe's men to build a duct from a stream to bring in clean water and one to take out the foul. During this work, the men were so busy that the fights and brawls all but stopped. As soon as the duct work was complete, most of the signs of ill health in the tribe stopped. The high priest's young son had been one who fell ill time after time and once almost died. Soon after the duct was built, he got well and stayed well. The high priest was sure the Christian priest had healed his son. From that day on, he did not thwart the Christian priest's plans.

Once the men were done with the duct work, though, they went back to their wine. It was as if life had not changed. The Christian priest again took a close look at the way the tribe lived it. It was plain to see that being drunk caused the brawls and Justin found that the men were bored which led them to drink. Each of their wives would talk trash about her "weak" man and then begin on all the other men of the tribe. This trash talk led to more brawls among the men and fights among the families. Things in the tribe seemed to just get worse and worse.

He found that the men were bored since they had no source of work. They lived by going on hunts for food, and the women found plants to eat in the fields and woods. *This was not good for peace*, he thought. *They are still a wild tribe.*

Once a week, he watched each man race his horse for fun and to win bets from friends. The tribe's old men would rate the horse on its speed and strength. A man was held in high praise and fame if he won and his horse then judged the best. In fact, this tribe's god was a horse god. Each man's goal was to trade for or breed his horse until he had one that would win the race. In truth, each horse in the tribe would win when they were raced next to a horse from any other tribe.

Justin thought he might fail in the task that Gregory had given him. Then one day as he stood near the race track, he watched the Equites Romani from that part of Gaul come to race their mounts against the tribe's. Justin saw that when a tribe's horse was raced next to a Roman horse, the tribe's horse would not fail to win. All at once God put a hint of a plan in his mind. *Why not?* he thought The tribe liked to breed top mares with the best studs to yield prize colts. They were proud of these colts and held on to them. At no time in the past would they trade the colts to other tribes and of course not to Rome. They did not want the mounts to be used against them in war. Since they were now a part of Rome, this rule made no sense.

Justin talked to the chief about a change. After he thought about it for a few days and talked with his priest, the chief gave the green light to Justin's plan. He made a new rule for the tribe. The tribe would now breed, raise, and sell mounts to the Roman troops. Justin asked Pope Gregory to get the Roman Magister Equitum to purchase the mounts from the tribe for Roman troops in Gaul.

The Romans loved the tribe's mounts and wanted more. Then a shift in the tribe's way of life began. It took only a month or two to see a change. As the tribe sold the young mounts, they were paid a great deal. The tribe's wealth grew, and their fame in Gaul grew as well. They worked so hard that they stopped their brawls. When night came, they spent much time in talks about their day's tasks and plans for the next. The men and boys of tribes who lived near the war tribe were hired to help with the new trade. With these good times, good will grew among the tribes.

With their new wealth, the tribe could buy the best seeds and sow them for food. The wives did not have to roam to find plants to eat. Fields were full of crops. In fact, some of the wives hired the poor to work in their fields while they kept the family's books. The wives still talked about their men but did not trash talk them . . . much. Justin's change had brought peace to the homes as well.

As the tribe changed for the good, Justin led both the tribe's chief and priest to Christ. The rest of the tribe were swift to seek and find Christ as their Lord. In a few years, five young men pledged to be trained as Christian priests. The tribe cheered and cried with joy at the news.

Through the thoughts, acts, and love of a young priest, a fiery war tribe found a deep peace and joy from their faith in Christ. And they were fierce no more.

19

THE ROAD AHEAD

Liz Kimmel

Guam is a jewel of an isle, set alone in the sea not far from the Philippines. It is bright and warm, an Eden on Earth today. Coral reefs wrap it like a belt and serve as home to fish so full of color, whose size and shape offer a mix as vast as the ocean. One of the things I loved best was to dive in this deep water and search out thrills for my eyes to savor. I made my home on Guam for a brief bit of time. And it might well have been the place of my death, if not for the grace of God.

I lived near the top of a high hill in Yoña and shopped in the city of Hagatña. In order to get from one place to the other I had to drive a very scary route. I coursed along this road many times and knew it well — but I had never liked it. The drive up the hill was not bad. I could hug the inner wall of the cliffs and not think about what lay below. But it was the drive down that caused me to worry. No rails were there to keep me from going over the edge, no guard to shield me from the steep and rocky fall that would have ended my life for sure. Even in the best of times, I had never felt safe on that trip into town. If I could have, I would have closed my eyes the whole way down.

That day I had things to do in Hagatña. With list in hand, I set out to reach my goals. The first clue that I was in peril came as I pressed on my brakes and tried to slow to a stop at the red light ahead of me. But the brakes were gone! My car had failed me. I tried not to panic. I lay on the horn and hoped that no one would hit me as I picked up speed and shot my way past those stopped at the light. I had made it through the first trial in one piece, but the worst was yet to come. I still couldn't stop. All I could do was hope that I would come out of this alive.

I held my breath — too scared even to pray. My mind was a total blank. I knew I had to come up with a plan, or I would soon be dead. I didn't know what to do. Then, things only got worse. I was struck blind! Plumes of white smoke began to pour from under my hood and hid the road from my sight. I feared that my car might be on fire —which caused me then to wish I could plunge over the cliff into the ocean. Yet how could I in a car and from such a height? But the thought did force my mind to "see" what was up ahead of me. In my mind's eye, I saw each curve ahead. *This next one is wide right, and after that, a slight angle to the left. Drive a little more, and the road goes to the right again.* My eyes were of no use to me. I might as well have closed them. But in my mind, I could trace the path. At the same time, I had to block out the sounds of the other cars' brakes and horns. As I wound my way toward the foot of the hill, I pumped my brakes (even though I knew it would not help) and blared my horn to warn others of the mess I was in.

I was so caught up in the fear that I couldn't think of what else I could do to stop my plunge. I hoped I wouldn't hit any other car. *Should I try to inch over to the other side of the road and nudge the wall of the cliff? What if a car was in that lan,e and I struck them head-on?* My speed knew no bounds, and my fear level rose with each added tick on the gauge. *Oh, God, what should I do? How do I get through this? I don't want to die, and I don't want to cause any other souls to die.*

I can't say for sure how I made it through all those curves — blind and with no brakes. I think an angel must have helped me steer the car when I could not. I felt the road start to level out. And then it came to me that I could use the shift lever to slow my speed. I pushed in the clutch and moved from fourth gear to third, then to second. I was going to make it! Down one more gear, and soon I was stopped. I inched my car door open and stepped out onto solid ground, dazed and stunned to see that I was still alive.

I'd like to say that I never drove that route again. But I did and each time made sure that the brakes on my car were in top form so that I would never ever have to drive that road by inner sight again.

Even though my eyes could not sense which way to go, I had a Guide who had never left me alone. I hadn't been sure how to pray, yet He still heard my heart's cry. And He brought me out of my very tight space into a firm, safe place. That day, the road had been filled with fright. But now I know that I can trust God to keep me safe on any road ahead.

20

IN THE DARK

Susan Thogerson Maas

The bell rang, and class was over. I had begun my first term at Oregon State University, and I loved it. But now I looked out and saw the sky start to grow dark. Wait. Not yet. Could night fall so soon? I shoved my books into my pack.

The time change. Why did I not think of "fall back" when I signed up for a late class? Psych 131: The Psychology of Human Emotions. I thought it might help me. But now I wasn't sure. I dashed for the door, but too late. Night had come. And with it the fear.

The fear had begun when I was eight years old and got lost in the woods. The trail had lured me by ferns and tall trees. The cool shade felt so nice on a warm day. But then the clouds rolled in as night came. I was lost and alone. No Mom or Dad to take me back to camp. I had stood there, ice in my heart, and screamed for them. Over and over I cried out, but no one heard. I sank to the damp ground, eyes wide and my voice gone. All was still. Well, not quite all. Was that creak a ghost? That howl a wolf? In the dark, how could I know? All night I'd lain there, eyes open, mind filled with dread.

When the light came, I cried out once more, and this time a voice called back. At last I was safe. But I was not the same. The next day all was well. But at night the fear came back. From then on, Mom had to leave on a lamp in my room at night. Even now, years later, in my dorm room, I slept with a night light.

And now I had let dark come upon me. The walk back to the dorm was long, and I had no one with me. I felt like such a baby.

But the dread crept deep into my heart and would not let go. Down the path I went, one slow step at a time. My heart beat like a drum, and I couldn't catch my breath. I felt as if I might faint. One block, then two. Small lamps lit the path, but they could not hold back the dark. It pressed in on me like a heavy weight. Still a ways to go. Would I make it? Tears came to my eyes.

My feet would move no more. I stood still in the black, black night. And the words squeezed through my lips. "Please, God. Help me."

Look up, child. I felt the words in my soul. Inch by inch I raised my head until I saw the sky — and gasped in awe. Tons of stars, so bright and pure, shone like gold in the dark night. A verse came to me: "The light shines in the darkness, and the darkness has not overcome it" (John 1:5, NIV). Yes, of course. A light that shines even in the night. Bit by bit, fear let go of my heart as I let God's light fill it. I took a deep breath, and a small laugh slipped out. How could I have been so blind?

I heard the pound of feet and turned to see a girl from my dorm. "Hi, Susan," she said. "How are you?"

"How am I?" I glanced up at the night sky one more time. "I'm great."

And I was. I knew the fear would come back, but now I was not alone. God had cleared away all clouds and shown me the stars.

21

Beatlemania –
Indianapolis, 1964

Darlene S. Mackey

When I woke up, my first thought was: *This is going to be the best day I've ever had!* I was in love with Paul McCartney, and that day I would see him in the flesh. *Who knows, maybe I'll even meet him!* I couldn't sleep but I could dream.

I was an easy child. I would do what mom said with no back talk. Mom would speak, and I would obey. But this was the Beatles. She had said I could go. JoAnne's brother was going to take us but couldn't get leave. Mom knew we were taking the bus, but I told her that Lita had done it before. She hadn't. I made my brother buy JoAnne's brother's seat so we wouldn't be out the extra five bucks. My brother was 12; we were 15, 16, and 17, and he was going with us. Jimmy was a big part of the plan. He would carry my Brownie Instamatic. I knew that I would have to scream a lot, and it's hard to scream and take pix. Yes, I knew I was going to be one of *those*.

Jimmy and I rose early and got ready for the Big Day. We left in time to walk the two blocks to where we would meet my two friends, JoAnne and Lita, then catch the first city bus to the Greyhound depot. It was simple; we bought just one-way fares, and the agent said the bus would drop us at the state fair right on the way. We didn't ask how to get back. We didn't care.

As the end of the first show came near, the crowd in front of the venue began to get very large. A high pitch of ardor had built up. We all loved the Beatles. We all were dying to see them as they left, to get as close as we could. Most of us would never have a chance like that again. That day was ours to spend with the Beatles. We were all on fire!

The three of us — only three since Jimmy did not get a vote — told each other that the first exit we came to wouldn't be the way the Beatles would come out since they wouldn't be able to get through so many fans. So we began to walk to the other side. On that side was a door with a window. A few fans were there, but it was quiet. Then through the door came Ringo. We saw him so we three girls did what any fan would do...SCREAM! So right away, an aide pulled Ringo back in. We were not alone. Our screams made some other fans aware and a few more began to come to the area.

That's when Jimmy began to stand by the door Ringo had come out. He didn't cause a fuss, so no one paid him any mind. Jimmy told us later that Ringo had stood in his safe place on the other side of the glass door and made faces at him. He thought Ringo was very funny. When Jimmy told me this, I was so glad that he had been the one with the Kodak, so that we could all see the great shots he had taken that no one else would have. But not so! Jimmy took no shots. Not one! For a long while later, every time I thought about it, I felt angry at him. But, I still had to be nice to him since he was my brother, and he did save me the five bucks for the extra seat.

The pace began to step up. Cops come and began to form two lines, Every other man faced out, and the one next to him faced in and then they locked arms. Three or four cars had parked at the end of that line. When they were all in place, the door opened again, and this time the Beatles rushed out. First came John, then George.

At that point, with no time to think, I dove for the line and went right through. (I wouldn't know until later that Lita went through at the same time.) John and George ran, and I ran with them. George was right in front of me. I touched his back, then put my hand on his arm. He turned back toward me, and from the look on his face, I think he thought I might hurt him. Never! I reached out and put my full open hand on his hair, and that was when I felt a grip on my neck.

With one hand, a cop had grabbed me by the throat, lifted me off the ground, and threw me to the grass. Even so, I couldn't get over how lucky I felt. I thought it had to be a dream. Only in a dream could I touch George. YES!

The Beatles and their group got in the cars and were gone before too many fans even knew they had been there. (No, Jimmy still did not snap even one photo.)

When they left, I pulled up a tuft of grass from where they went through the lines. (I still have it.) Then we again walked to the back of the venue where a huge crowd still surged about a bunch of lined-up limos. Even then, we guessed that the limos had been staged as a decoy to make the fans think that the Beatles were on their way out. Bands did come out that way, but only the less-loved ones. As I and my friends knew, the Beatles were gone.

We began to tell our story since we had become part of the drama. I had touched the Beatles so the fans tried to touch me. It was a bit scary for a while, but with each new wave of fans came to touch us, we got more and more used to it. I planned to never wash that hand again, but I did. Hands get dirty. Even a girl of 15 knows that.

Some fans there told us how to get to the bus depot in Indianapolis so that we could get home. Once there, I told mom all that had gone on. She wasn't very happy, but she wasn't angry. I had to tell her, since the last time she had seen me, I didn't have a black-and-blue print of a hand on my neck.

Good thing I told her, too, since the news that night played film of the event at the fair. And there I was, right on TV, going through the line, touching George, and being thrown out! Only when I saw that film did I find out that Paul had been right there next in line after George. Paul — the love of my life!

If only I had known to stop and turn, we could have met.

22

THE PLAZA

Michael Reynolds

It was Christmas eve and I stood in the Faith Baptist Church of Abilene TX where I saw a van with the words, "Abilene Christian University" pull up to the door. From it, six girls piled out. When I saw the first girl to walk in, I caught my breath. She smiled at me, this drab out-of-place geek who was more at home with Africa's snakes, bugs, and tall grass than sharp girls. I tried to speak, but where do vocal cords go when you need them the most?

Traci held out her hand and said, "Hi, I'm from ACU. Are you new here?" I was still at a loss for words. Then some part of my brain came to life so I could say, "My grandfather is the pastor, and I'm here for Christmas."

"Why don't you sit with us?" she asked as she waved to the others from the van. I had grown up in Africa while my parents served at a church mission there, so I well knew the sting of fire ants, the screech of monkeys, and the chills of malaria; but what I felt as I sat with Traci that night was all new to me.

I began to learn that Traci felt like a fish out of water in America as well. A military brat, she had lived most of her life in Germany. Like me, her American blood cells and DNA still didn't help her fit into the U.S. We both felt out of place in our home land.

Our love took off with phone calls, mail, and my visits to her school. At the heart of our love was the strength we found in each other as an alien in American skin. We felt that God had made us like two gears of a clock that mesh in space and time.

Our honeymoon took us to her Germany. In Berchtesgaden we

sat in a plaza and talked of days to come. She loved that place and all the good times she shared there with her mom and dad. Her German past — with its easy way of life, the art on the streets, and the awe of the Alps — held deep roots in Traci's soul. Yet with each sip of latte, she voiced her new dreams — of our days to come in the US and her plan for kids, a home, good jobs, and close friends.

At the time, in that quaint small town by the Alps, we did not know that cancer cells in Traci's body had formed a plan of their own. After four months back in the U.S., we found out that she was sick.

Three years have gone now, since our latte and dreams in the plaza. I could not help but come back to this spot and think of her, honor her, cry for her. It was here that we spun our dreams with each other and our alien values found their rest in our hopes. Six months ago, as she was dying, her last words to me were, "Please, visit the plaza and think about us."

23

Play It Again

Jeanetta Chrystie

Claire, Gail and Anne filled the couch.

"What's the hold up? Start the show!" Claire said with a bit of a whine in her voice.

They each grabbed snacks and Cokes as Anne clicked *Play*. She loved this time with her friends, girl time to just sit and watch as the hours passed.

Anne sat still as *Gone With The Wind* played on her big screen. Rhett scooped up his bride and pranced up the stairs.

Anne glanced at the pile of M&Ms in her palm, sighed, and popped them into her mouth.

"Never in a month of Sundays," she said aloud.

Her friends shushed her. Claire rolled her eyes.

"Why not?" Gail mouthed.

Anne thought about what to say. *Can I claim that Rhett is not my type? No. Our front stairs are too small? No. It's best to just keep my mouth shut.*

Truth be told, Anne felt fat. She wasn't. Mae West curves, yes; but not fat.

She looked down, then poured a pile of M's into her hand and stared at them.

After a glance at the screen, she picked out a green M and ate it. She liked the green ones best. She knew that they all tasted the same, yet green still *seemed* to taste best.

Four hours flew by. Soon it was time for Claire and Gail to meet their Friday night dates. Anne walked them out her door, through the front doors, and down the front stairs. They left in Gail's car.

As Anne turned to climb the stairs, her foot slipped off the last step and she fell in a heap on the ground. She lay still, groaned, and tried to stretch out flat on her back.

"May I help you, Miss?" drawled a deep, male voice.

"Thanks, I think my foot's hurt." Her voice cracked, so she gave him a quick nod and smiled.

A wall of a man scooped her up in his arms as if she were a sack of feed — with curves.

Anne looked at his face: his head full of short, blond curls, his trimmed beard, and his blue eyes that smiled back at her.

'too bad my place is on the first floor, she thought as she placed her hands on his arm.

"I'm Brett," he said as he climbed three steps.

"Yes, we've met. My name is Anne."

She had seen him come and go from door five at the far end of the first floor. He had seemed shy at Grey House's meet-and-greets.

As he stepped through the front door, she said, "Mine is the first door on the right. I share it with my friend Beth." She showed him the key in her other hand.

With her still in his arms, he took the key from her hand, put it in the lock, and turned it. The soft click let the door swing in. Brett set her down on the couch. The *Gone With the Wind* DVD showed its main screen. He smiled.

Then, Beth and Joe came through the front door and rushed in the open door of their place. Beth glanced at the room.

"Where are Claire and Gail?" she frowned.

"We had a great time. They just left for their dates. I fell on the front step and hurt my foot," Anne said, "This is Brett from down the hall. He helped me back in."

Beth smiled. "Nice."

Anne didn't think Beth meant her hurt foot.

Joe shook Brett's hand, "Where do you work?"

While the guys talked, Beth grabbed a first aid cold pack from the fridge.

"This is a good movie," Brett said with a nod at the screen. "Shall I call for take-out food?"

Anne smiled, and with a glance at Beth said, "Yes, Thai for four".

Beth cleaned up the snacks. Joe pulled up three more chairs since Anne's legs and hurt foot took up the rest of the couch. They all talked. Soon, the food came. Joe and Brett paid for the food and sat down to watch *Gone With The Wind*.

For the next four hours, while the rest of them kept their eyes fixed on the screen, Anne watched Brett, not Rhett.

24

HOWLER

Debra Pierce

My friend Lynn is a CNA at an old folks home. One day, Lynn told me a about a ninety-six-year-old woman named Marge who lived there. She was a small, thin woman with sky blue eyes, and a crown of snow-white hair. She had lost her husband, Fred, a long time ago. And they never had a child. Marge called where she had come to live her "stop-over home," the place she would wait until God called her to her real home.

"God blessed me with a love for dogs," Marge told Lynn. "And He blessed me with a gift to teach." The home didn't allow dogs to live there, but on Wednesdays, a dog was brought in for Pet Therapy day. On these days, which Marge called, "pat-the-dog day," her eyes would glow. When wheeled over to Duke — a large, brown hound with ridged fur on his back — Marge would place her hands on the sides of his face and stare into his eyes. The dog would nudge and lick her hand. Then Marge would say, "Duke, you look just like my dog, Howler. I used to walk Howler in the woods near my house, but that was a long time ago. Oh, how I loved those walks with Howler!" Marge would pause and look off into her past. Then she would pat Duke's head with, "Soon, Howler will come back to take me to heaven." The first time Lynn heard this, she asked Marge why she had said it.

"Oh dear, don't you know? Psalm 37:4 says 'Delight yourself in the Lord and He will give you the desires of your heart.' And what my heart wants is to walk through those woods with Howler and have him lead me to heaven." Marge thought that when we die God brings us back to a time in our lives that filled us with joy.

Then we go to heaven. This was the hope Marge held on to while she lived at the home. No one tried to tell her that it might not be true. When her church friends came to see Marge, they did not talk about what *they* thought about Marge's thoughts — at least not since the day when they left Marge's room and one of them brought it up. Lynn was in the hall and heard one woman say, "Jesus is Marge's Savior. To me, that's all that counts. The way Marge gets to heaven… well let's just leave that up to God."

Lynn told me that when Marge stared into Duke's eyes and spoke to him, she glowed. Her eyes got bright, and her joy filled the room. Then Marge would delve into her past and bring it all back to life. Most of what Marge shared had to do with her dog, Howler. She told her tales to Duke. "You know how Howler got his name? When he was just a pup all he did was howl. He just had a lot to say. Fred and I used to howl back at him!" Marge laughed when she told Duke this. "Old Man Clarke, as he was known in town, told folks he was scared there was a wolf in the woods who would kill his cows. So when we'd to go buy corn, Fred and I would take Howler to the farm with us to put Old Man Clarke's mind at ease. Howler liked the cows. One day when I couldn't find Howler, Old Man Clarke called to tell me that Howler was in his cow field and had gone to sleep next to one of his cows! After that, Fred called Howler "The Dog that Sleeps with Cows." The tales Marge told Duke made the staff smile.

As time went by, Marge's heart grew weak, too weak for her to get out of bed. She lost weight. And she would not eat. But her eyes still glowed when Duke was brought to her room. He would rest his head on her lap as Marge would stroke it and say, "Soon, Duke, Howler will come get me and bring me to heaven." The last time Marge saw Duke she told him about when Howler was gone for hours so she called Old Man Clarke to see if Howler was with his cows. He told her that he saw Howler at Fred's grave. "When it was Howler's time to die, that is where I found him," Marge said, her eyes moist with tears. She paused in the grip of her grief. "I've waited for Howler a long, long time so I can see Fred." She sighed. "Tell Howler to come soon." Duke whined. Then he barked. The next day, Marge's life came to a close.

The hour when Marge died, Lynn was at the end of her shift. On the way to Marge's room she told me she thought she heard a dog howl. Then when she went into the room, she saw Marge stroke her lap and say with a smile, "Howler, you've come!" Then she closed her eyes. When her shift was over, Lynn saw a car from the dog pound in the lot and a woman on the grounds. "Some folks who live near here called us about a stray dog," she told Lynn. "At first they thought it was a wolf — since they heard it howl. But then they saw it and said it was some kind of a hound. I can see its tracks in the snow, heading over there." The woman walked to where the prints led — Marge's room. Then she came back to Lynn. "The dog tracks just end," she said. "With so much sun in that area, the snow has melted so I lost my trail. 'seems the dog may have run off into those woods. 'guess I'll go check that out."

"I didn't tell the woman that the dog would never be found," said Lynn. Then with a pause, Lynn smiled and said, "Delight yourself in the Lord and He will give you the desires of your heart."

25

ANGEL FALLS

Ken Proctor

God must love my son. More than once He has reached
out — or sent an angel in His stead — to shield Timothy,
from harm. Take the time a few years back when Tim and friends
set out for Oneonta Falls.

It was a warm spring day that wooed Tim and a few pals out for
a nice hike in the Columbia River Gorge. Portland thinks of the
gorge — only an hour away from home — as Mother Nature's
gift to the Pacific Northwest, right here in our own back yard.
Laced with snow-fed creeks and etched by well-kept trails, the
slopes lie heavy with the scent of fir trees, damp moss, and ferns.
Black-tailed deer haunt the woods' edge like gray shades at night
to graze on berry canes and vine-maple leaves, while wild rams
and ewes skip about the rocky cliffs and crags, by day. All in all,
it's a great place for four young men to spend a late-spring day.

They chose the Oneonta Falls Trail, on the Oregon side with
views of the wide Columbia River below, and snow-capped Mt.
St. Helens to the north. Short but steep, the dirt trail starts at
the car-park jump-off point and winds its way up into the lush
green fir stands that line Oneonta Creek. This course of water
spills and churns its way down from the rock-faced bluffs above,
through its own tight, water-cut slot gorge before it melds into
the Columbia. A fine hike. A good choice.

But was it? Wet with the rains that keep the slopes lush, the
rocks mossy, and muddy spots slick; the trail is a good place to
slip and land on the back of your front. Signs nailed along the
way tell the wise to keep to the trail, avoid steep edges, and stay

safe. But young men can't read. Or they don't. And these guys didn't — or at least they didn't take heed.

"Hey, let's get a photo," they said. "Over here, in the light." All four stepped out along a rocky ledge above the creek with the vista at their backs, the sun on their hair, and grins on their young faces. Click. "Take two. Smi-i-ile." Click. "Cool."

"Hey — Where's Tim?"

Due to one wrong step and one loose clump of muddy, mossy soil that looked more solid than it was, my son had slid right off the trail. Head first, then butt first, then every which way, Tim flailed at the brush as he flew by. The mist-damp slope had turned into a rock-strewn Slip-n-Slide that came to a halt where it dropped eighteen feet straight down into Oneonta Gorge.

But Tim didn't. Halt, that is. Tim's chums watched as he plunged into the snow-cold, rock-choked sluice just yards from the point where water met sky — the top of Oneonta Falls. They blanched as their buddy was swept away, to plunge over the edge.

"Oh, crap! Let's go!" The three men raced back down the hill, fully aware they could not get to Tim in time to help. But they knew they had to try.

This is the part where the angel stepped in. Or swooped in. Oneonta Falls stands over sixty feet high, from its cleft lip to the thin, rocky pool at its base. A stone-cold killer if ever there was one. A death trap with time-worn teeth that wait to bite, to bash skulls, to break bones.

But not that day. Not my son. One small part of the pool lies deep and rock free — one wee place to land with a hope to see the next day. And Tim found it. Not a clean dive, mind you. No style points. It wouldn't have scored high with the Russian judge. But he hit it. Spot on.

Still, he wasn't in the clear yet. Oneonta Creek spat Tim out as if he were a sour grape — only banged, bruised, sliced and diced, soaked, half drowned, and ice-cold chilled to the bone. As he clawed his way toward shore, he found an angel. Four of them, in fact — a whole team of paramedics out for a hike on their one day off. As they stood at the base of the falls, they had seen the whole thing. Slip, slide, yelp, flight, fall, and sploosh.

The well-versed team knew what to do. They'd packed the right kits and all the right gear. And they flew to his aid. While three worked to get Tim warmed up, one called for help. By the time Tim's friends reached him there on the gravel beach, the team had him wrapped up and ready for a long trip to the ER.

In the end — after a bunch of nicks, cuts, bumps, and bruises — Tim had gone over Oneonta Falls and lived. When he shouldn't have. He walked away with soggy money, a dead cell phone, and only minor harm — to pride. A small price to pay, I'd say. It should have been far worse.

But God loves my son, and He has the power to save.

26

SAME TRAIN, SAME SEAT, SAME VIEW

Andrea Woronick

I woke up to the sound of my phone's ping. It was the kind of day that made me want to stay in bed with the sheets pulled up over my head. The sky was a bleak gray, the winds cold, and I sensed the rain to come. I did not want to get up, but I did and dressed for work. The long train ride in would give me some time to rest. I made some tea, grabbed my cup, and rushed out the door.

I stepped onto the train, walked to the back of the car, sat down and put my bag on the seat next to me. It was like most days — the same train, the same seat, the same view. I watched as the train filled up. Most who came on the train were on their way to work, and I see them each day. Most, that is, but not her. I watched. I knew she would be there soon. I couldn't think of a day when she had not come. And, just as the train warned that the doors were to close, she stepped on.

She glanced at me and took a seat on the left side of the train. She looked out on the tracks, as she did most days. Her crimped shirt and worn jeans told me that she was not dressed for work. She looked so sad. She did not smile or speak. She just gazed out through the glass as the train sped down the tracks.

I closed my eyes for a bit but woke up when the train came to a stop. I took hold of my bag and saw that she had stood up to leave the train. I glanced out to see the same sight that I saw each day at that stop: the old man with the small boy by his side, their hands locked. She stepped down off the train. With a nod to the old man, she bent down and held her arms wide to the boy. He ran to her, and they hugged. She held on tight, but the boy did not seem to mind. Her eyes were shut as tears ran down her face, just as they did each day. In a bit, the three of them strolled down the street. Then I lost sight of them.

Later, from my stop, I walked the four blocks to my job, sat down at my desk, and viewed the stack of work that I had to get through. My mind was not on my work, though; it was on the scene at that train stop. Who is she? Why does she take the train at the same time each day? Who is the small boy that she meets?

The next day, I again woke up to the sound of my phone's ping. This day won't be the same, I thought. I decided to delay so I could board the train after the woman. Then I will take the seat next to her, and when the train starts to move, I will find the nerve to speak, tell her my name, and ask what hers is, I plan. I will try to be a friend. She looks as though she needs one. Will she talk to me? Will she tell me who the man and the boy are? Will she let me into her world?

I got up, dressed for work, and headed for the train. When I got there, I did not board but held back to wait. My plan was all set. By the end of the day I would know more — at least who she is. This would be a good day, I might have a new friend.

I had to wait and wait and wait, but she did not come. Just as the doors began to close, I hopped on the train. Where is she? The next day when I went to the train, I did not see her.

In fact, I have not seen her since. What changed? I did not get to know her or be her friend, but I do think of her each day as I board the train for work. My hope is that she is with the small boy that she rode the train to meet, the boy she hugged so tight. As the train starts to move down the track I think, So much is the same and yet so much is not, for she is not here.

27

Soap Opera Story

Alice Murray

As a J.D. I have a staid and quiet job, right? I read big books and use big words at my big desk. No, that's not me. I help folks to adopt and gain a child. The quest for a wee one often takes me away from my desk and out into the big wide world where an odd thing or two might occur. And one day the odd thing for me was an event that could have been a soap-opera story line.

The first clue that I was in for a wild ride was the name of the woman who came to me for help. It was the same as the name of a role on a hit soap opera. No joke! And her name only gave a small clue as to what her life was like. Yes, a soap. The woman — let's call her Jane — had a husband, and she was with child. But Jane told me that her husband was not the father of her baby. She'd had a fling while on a trip out of state, and this was that other man's baby. She did not plan to tell her husband that she was with child. Jane would keep it under wraps. I did not know how she would do this since she lived with her husband, and they slept in the same bed. Jane was a thin girl, and a baby bump would be easy to spot or feel. She had not gone to see an M.D. in order to keep her being with child on the down low.

One day I came to work happy that it was my last day on the job prior to a trip out of town. With no one to meet with, I knew that would have a quiet day at my desk. Then the phone rang. I was told that Jane was on the phone and was upset. Not only was Jane upset; she was in labor. And she had no way to get to the

ER. Could I give her a ride? Of course, I would go save the day and give her a lift. Her house was not far from my place of work. But, just as our call was to end, Jane told me that her husband was home. She had made up a story about going to check out a new job and talk with a man who might be her new boss. Jane asked that I play along with this plan. What could I say?

As I drove to Jane's house, I was in hopes that her husband would not come out or try to speak to me. But, no. Who came to the door upon my knock but Jane's husband. I told him that I was there to pick up Jane. I was in fear that he would ask me where I was going with Jane. I did not want to lie. Jane came to the door, and I did not have to talk to her husband any more. Jane had on sweat pants. What job did her husband think she could get with such pants on?

Out to the car we went and off to the ER a few miles away. Once Jane was in the car, all would be good, right? Wrong! Jane began to yell as we drove down the road. She said that the baby was going to come — then! A series of thoughts flew through my mind: *No, not in my car! Would my boss pay to clean up my car if the baby was born in it?* I told Jane to hold on. "Cross your legs! Don't think about it." Jane began to huff and puff and yell more. I drove fast up to the ER door. Jane got out of my car and told me to leave. *What? How can I just dump her off at the door and leave her at the curb in great pain?* But I did as I was told.

Back to work I went. Soon I got a call that Jane's baby had been born; it was a girl. The baby had come very soon after Jane got to the ER. The other news was that Jane had been on drugs, so the baby was in the NICU. At that point, no one could keep Jane's husband in the dark. At least I didn't have to tell him the news about his wife. The other J.D. at work had that fun job. The husband had never guessed that Jane had been with child. He just knew that the baby was his, so a DNA test was done. And, as it turned out, he was the father of the baby. Now that her husband knew and it was his baby, Jane did not want to place the baby for a family to adopt her. What about the nice man and his wife whom we had lined up to adopt the child? How could we call them and dash their dream of being a mom and dad?

Not happy that Jane had taken drugs while with child, the state was going to take the baby and put her in a state home. At that point, we had Jane, her husband, the nice man and his wife, and the state — all after the baby. It was a tug of war! Would the baby be okay? Who would get her? Would Jane and her husband stay as husband and wife after this event? Would the nice folks get a wee one? Would I stay sane? Cue the soap music. Did I tell you that I love my job? It is never dull. In fact, it is often a real-life soap opera.

28

THANK YOU, JESUS AND PANCHO VILLA!

Susanna Shutz Robar

Raymond Leigh Reid was a get-it-all-out-there kind of guy, a bold and brave soul. Yet, as he grew up in Iowa, he was also quick to show some meek and mild points along with a sense of humor that was all but dull. In school, Ray learned how to copy down what people said in a very fast way. His skill found him a job on the Twentieth Century Limited Train which ran from Chicago to New York and back.

In 1902, at the age of twenty-one, Ray was a one-man steno pool. His task was to take notes from the likes of John D. Rockefeller, J.P. Morgan, and Andrew Carnegie. He wrote their clear, rich thoughts by hand. Then he would sit in the last car of the train to type up the notes on his Remington and get them ready to mail at the next train stop.

Yet Ray yearned to know more of the world. His heart was set on Mexico, a land still full of *vaquero*s and brash feats of pluck and guts. Ray had been born in 1882 when the era of the wild American west had just begun to wane. This brought the rise of tall tales that would thrill and stir most minds to dream — as it did for young Ray. He had heard tales about foul men such as Jesse James, Sam Bass, Curly Bill, the Younger clan, and the Apache Kid. But Ray's heart was stirred more by the lives of those on the right side of the law: Bat Masterson, Heck Thomas, Virgil and Wyatt Earp, and the Texas Rangers. Ray knew that both groups of men had wills of steel to tear down the law on the one hand or to hold the law up high on the other.

The tales of these men drove, or in fact pushed, Ray over the Arizona state line and south into Mexico. His plan was to take a train ride to Cananea, Sonora, Mexico and work as a steno for his uncle in the ore mines. He also had plans to wed a girl with dark eyes along the way, and live there for the rest of his years.

At first light one day in 1906 Ray put on a three-piece suit: pants, white shirt, vest and coat to match, as well as a smart bow tie. With a straw hat on his head and a cane in hand, he bade fare-thee-well to his parents and young siblings Then, in his nice, new suit, he got on that train bound for Mexico and began his quest for a new life.

Ray was a fair, just, and kind man, who hoped for the same kind of care from other folks. For this cause, from the start, he went to work right next to the rough men who cut the rock face. In time, Ray was to step up in rank as foreman, then as clerk to his uncle, Colonel William Greene of the Cananea Consolidated Copper Company. But Ray took time to make good friends with all in the town. And he would share tales meant to amaze and excite them — true tales of feasts and camps, fights and stab wounds, bad jokes, mine strikes, and stews into which no one would want to jump. He told tales of horse rides at the end of day with the town's head law man, and more.

At this time, Mexico was in a state of near chaos. A ground swell gave rise to the Revolution of 1910. Yet Ray was true to his uncle in Cananea, until his uncle met with early death when crushed under the wheels of a horse-drawn coach. Even with his uncle gone, Ray still held to his Mexican dream.

Then, on a Monday in the spring of 1912, General Emilio Campa's men came close to Villa Verde Station. Ray, who was on leave from work, was with the *vaqueros* who were to move a herd in the same area. At about 9:00 A.M., Ray and two other Americans, Abe Jesson and Oscar Simms, were with W.W. Wilkey's men from Cananea. Each rode his own horse at the rear of a herd of 700 steers from the Bacanuchi Ranch. The *vaquero* at the far rear came to Oscar and told him that a rebel group was to their west. Oscar left. Ray and Abe thought he had gone for a fresh horse. But in next to no time they could smell a rat; Oscar had gone to the rebel men. Ray and Abe made a quick turn to Cerro San José.

As soon as Ray and Abe made the turn, General Campa's men took 10 shots that set all to flight. Three men made a try to cut the Americans off to the right, and three to the left. Ray and Abe "went north like a streak of light!" They were able to out-fox the rebel men with an eighteen-mile swift-horse ride and a safe sleep in Naco, Sonora, Mexico.

Ray and Abe went back to their ranch jobs later that year, and never saw Oscar again. But in due time they were put to the test once more. This time they were out on a ride in their free hours one Sunday. Again, they were with the *vaqueros* at work with the herds. As they rode along, they could see a large band of men to the west. Then a large band of men came into sight to the east. As the groups drew near, Ray could see that the east band was the Rurales, an army set up by the Mexican rule; Francisco "Pancho" Villa led the west band. In a split atom of time, every "Gringo Americano" rode hard and fast. For thirty-two hours straight they fled "Pancho" Villa's blitz with the Rurales to reach safe land in Arizona. Ray never went back to his land of love and duty, his dear Mexico.

In spite of it all or due to it all, in 1918 in an Arizona town by the name of Duncan, Ray met his girl for life: a tall twenty-two-year-old who taught English to young ones. She had blue eyes, not dark, and a heart of gold. Ray found his gem, his pearl, his prize and was wed to her for fifty-two years until his death in 1971.

In one way, I value the man who was a rebel from the Mexican state of Chihuahua and who, on that Sunday in 1912, chose to press into the rough plains and chase Ray out of Mexico.

Had it not been for Pancho Villa's wish to run Ray out and God's ever-ready grace to keep him safe from harm, I would not be here to tell you this tale. Raymond Leigh Reid was my Grandpa.

Thank you, Jesus and Pancho Villa!

29

BACK THE WAY WE CAME

Frank Ramirez

We greet you, O Great One. Let us tell you our tale. Jerusalem fell.

The Great Temple was torn down in 587 BC, and it was no more. Our kin were killed or were made slaves or were sent off to far lands. Yet still we spoke the old words and sang the old songs.

In years long, long past we had been slaves in Egypt, but with God's help we were freed. Now some of us chose to go back. We fled to Egypt.

And there, at the fort in Yub, far to the south, we built a new shrine like to the old one. It had five gates like the old one. Our priests took up the old tasks. In this way we still praised God who was with us in a far-off land.

When those who hate us died, when the place known as The Gate of the Skies fell — just like our town once fell — we stayed in Egypt for it had proved home. We had our shrine. We praised God there. We stayed as the years went by, for our young ones grew and had young ones of their own.

Then, in in 420 BC, though Darius still reigned, those who hated us anew tore down our shrine in the town of Yub. They set all in flames -- the doors, the roof, all of it. The gold, and all else, they stole!

And so we beg you, O Great One, say that we might build our shrine once more. Let us praise God once more in our shrine, at the fort in Yub.

30

ONE DARK NIGHT

Angela Mattingly

The four of us had no idea what lay ahead as we drove over Bear Mountain in New York. My sister and I sat in the back and a friend of mine up front with her boyfriend, Mike, at the wheel. We were on a road trip from Texas to see our friend turn into a West Point grad. It had been a long trip, and now in the wee hours of a new day, the mood in the car was tense. To add fuel to the fire, my sister and I were at our wit's end due to Mike's laid-back ways which made him seem slow to think and slow to act.

Not for the first time that trip, there we were — stopped at a wide spot on the side of the road, in the dark. Mike's gaze was fixed on the map. The rest of us spied a black limo pull off to the edge of the road and park next to us. Out stepped the tall, thin dark man who had just parked the limo. Clad in all black, with both hands in his coat, he walked over to our car. Not a word crossed his lips. Mike, eyes still on the map, rolled down the glass to ask which way to go. The man just stood there. He turned and walked back to the limo, hands still out of sight, with never a word said. My sister and I were spooked by how the man acted. Soon after, Mike found his route, and we all talked about the strange event as we forged on.

Only a blink of time down the road, we made a turn to climb the next hill. All at once we saw a crazed young woman who shone a light in our eyes as she and two men rushed our car. They had blocked our lane, and a large box truck was parked in the other, so we couldn't pass. In front of the truck lay a man face down on the road. Even though we three girls begged Mike to keep going, he had no choice. Both sides of the road were blocked, so he could not yield to our pleas. He had to come to a stop.

The woman with the light ran to Mike's door. Her hands shook as if she were full of fear, but it was a fear that did not come off as real. Mike was slow to take in all the buzz at the scene, so he rolled down the glass to chat as my sister and I hit the floor of the car in panic.

I heard her scream a flood of words — that she had been on her way to get her man on a flight, that one man there was on his way home, and that we had to go a half mile down the road to a house on the right. She barked an order for us to turn right and go down a long, dark drive so we could ask to use their phone to call for help.

At this point, I crawled up from the floor to get a look at the scene. My eyes scanned for the man and the limo. He was not here. But still mid lane in front of the box truck was a man face down on the road; head turned toward the other ditch. He had on a clean white tee shirt and jeans. I could see his arms, laid out flat on the road above his head. His left leg was bent at the knee, foot in the air. His shin leaned on the front frame of the box truck with his toes under the brand badge of the truck. I saw no blood, no sweat, no maimed leg, no scuff or skid marks. His hair was not even out of place. And no one knelt at the man's side to offer care.

I turned to the woman at the car to learn more about the scene. "Where was the one who drove the truck?" I asked her. "Is that man alive?" "Do you know what took place here?" "How long have you been here?" I got no reply.

Things did not add up to me. If she had been off to get her guy on a flight, her car should have been in the other lane. Yet all on the scene were in the same lane as ours. Why hadn't one of those there gone that half mile down the road to make the call — since no one was busy at the man's side to give aid? Also how was it that they all knew of a house down the road that couldn't be seen for the many trees in the way? Just then, my sister and I both yelled at Mike to roll up his pane and get out of there. At that point, we didn't care how we got away, even if he had to run over them!

When the group heard Mike shift the car into drive, they moved. We did phone for help, but only after we found a pay phone many miles down the road. After the call, we pressed on with our trip, never to know the truth of what had come to pass on that far-from-quiet road one dark night.

31

STORY THIEF

David Shorts

Tuesday, October 11, 1966 is a day the Shorts family will not soon forget. On an old typed copy, faint red pen marks the date when my grandma, Ruby Okla Shorts, pitched a near hit to a book agent. She tried and tried to sell *Willow of the Stars* but with no luck. On October 11th, she went to Mimi's Café, which used to be a block south of USC, but I guess it was knocked down and flats were built in its place. In those days, she lived in Imperial Beach. The only way I've sent my work to agents is via email, but it seems that in 1966 many a writer would meet face to face with an agent. She sat with Will Groben, an agent, but her notes don't say whom he worked for.

"It was busy that day." She told us. She felt sweat on her palms as she sat with busy artsy-type folks. For many years, she had hoped for that big break. Over a light lunch she told her story of a far-away world and a meek farm boy named Willow who had skills in magic. His friends all joined the cause to fight the evil king and his army. When Willow was born, the evil king killed his father. Not only that, but the evil king had the same magic skills as Willow. The Ruler, as he was called, wore a black cape and cloak to cover all but his mouth. In the end, they fight an epic duel with fire swords. The Ruler cuts off Willow's hand and is ready to kill him. Then he stops. He says, "You didn't know your father, did you?" Willow says, "That's cuz you killed him!" Then the Ruler says, "No, Willow, I am your father." He asks Willow to join him to rule the world. Willow won't, uses magic to make his sword fly to his other hand and kills his father while tears roll down his cheeks. The world is set free from the curse of the evil king, and while cheers and peels of bells echo from city to city, Willow sets a pyre for the father he never knew.

After she had told him the gist of her story, Mr. Groben read the first ten pages or so. Grandma says that his exact words were, "Too much exposition in your prose." And he gave it back. That was the end of lunch, but as you may know, not the end of Grandma's story. Parts of that sound like a story most people know: "Star Wars." What I know is that George Lucas was at USC when my Grandma pitched her book, and eleven years later "Star Wars" was a movie. To make things worse, this was the second time her work had been ripped off. Years ago, she sent a poem she wrote to Edgar Albert Guest. The poem? *Myself.* It was in many of his books and is often called the worst great poem ever. We don't know how George Lucas heard the story, but he changed much of it. Guest didn't change a word.

32

GHOST

Pamela Rosales

M anda raised her hand, but Mrs. Cole didn't see it. She called on Kurt.

"X equals 23."

"Right," said Mrs. Cole.

Manda stared down at her paper. *Why? Why doesn't she see me?* Her straight brown hair fell to shield her face as a tear fell onto her paper. *Seventh grade, a new school, and I still feel like a ghost.*

The bell rang. Manda left the room apart from the other kids who joked and laughed as they made their way to the city bus stop for the ride home. She got on the bus, sat in the back next to an adult, and read a book. No one spoke. Her sister in eighth grade, Starla, sat in the front with a friend. Mike, Starla's twin, sat in the very last seat with a boy from his class. When the bus reached 10th Street, seven kids got off with Manda. Not one said hi or bye to her. She walked home with her sister and brother to the Vue Apartment.

"Hey, Mike, tell me about that guy who got off the bus with you. What's his name?" Starla asked.

"Why do you want to know?" he teased.

"Cause he's cute, that's why, dork!" Starla punched his arm.

After so many years of being tuned out, Manda knew not to try to join in their fun. Once home, the girls went to their room where ten-year-old Katy sat on her top bunk eating a candy bar.

"Katy-girl, get your clothes off the floor. This room is too small for you to have your stuff all over," Starla said.

"Bossy!" Katy shot back at her. Manda shared a room with

Starla and two other sisters: Katy in fifth grade and Lizzy in tenth grade. Mike shared a room with Joe Junior, now in 12th grade.

Mom didn't get home from work early enough to fix meals. Dad went straight from his day job to pump gas on Friday nights, so the kids were on their own for food this night. Mike and Starla raced to the fridge to grab the last two corn dogs. They went to their rooms to eat, then Manda looked for soup to heat up for Katy and her. Lizzy and Joe Junior weren't home yet.

While the kids kept busy with music, TV, and phone calls, Manda felt cut off from any human bond. The noise made it hard to focus on her book. She slipped into the half-bath to hide alone in pain. Hope-lost, teary eyes looked back at her. *Portland, a huge city, yet no one sees me. Home, school, bus, street, store — no one.* She pinched her arm. *Am I alive? I must be; I hurt inside and out.*

A plan began to take shape in her mind. "If no one knows I'm here, then no one will miss me when I'm gone," she spoke to her image in the mirror. "Maybe if I go far away I can start over." A news story about a child who flew to Rome prior to being found popped in her mind.

Saturday morning Manda got up, stuffed her clothes in a large Walmart bag, grabbed her $14 cash, and went out the door. Mom had to leave early on Saturdays to work at a 7-11. Dad would sleep until the P.M. Not one sibling took note as she left.

While Manda made her way onto the MAX train to Portland International Airport, she felt sure no one would take note of her or care. She got off the MAX and stayed close to groups with kids. Manda moved in and out of range so it wouldn't be clear which group she was with.

The TSA area looked hard to pass through. Manda watched to see if she could get an idea of how to make her way to the other side. After a while, a large high-school-band group neared the TSA line so she joined them. Her pulse throbbed. As she neared the agent, she looked to the side, bent down, and turned away to end up out of his sight — as usual. The fact that it worked did not shock her.

Manda then walked to a packed Southwest Airlines gate. Back near the wall, a crowd stood in two lines ready to board. Her whole body quaked as she joined the line. She again used her new skill to blend in and move past the agent onto the plane. *Please let there be an extra seat.*

An open middle seat near the back, with a man and woman on each side, looked safe. Manda sat, put her bag under the seat in front, and took deep gulps of air to calm down. She laid her coat over her chest and arms, closed her eyes and "slept" until the plane set down in Denver, Colorado, just over two hours later.

To Manda, it seemed that chaos reigned in the huge Denver International Airport. In panic, she looked left and right. Her plan had reached its end. The trip had only proved how out of sight she was. *What should I do? Oh God, if You are there, help me!* she begged. Manda saw a sign for the girls' room. She ran into a stall and sobbed. Fraught with fear, she let her sobs grow loud.

A knock on the stall door caused her to draw a sharp breath. "Are you all right?" a lady's voice asked.

"Yes," Manda squeaked.

"Can I help you?" the lady pressed.

"No!" she said, but Manda couldn't hold in her sobs.

Manda heard the lady ask, "Will you go get help?"

"Yes, I'll be right back," a voice said.

Back at the house, tired and worn, Mom dragged through the door after her eight-hour shift at 7-11. She plopped down on the couch, lay her head back, and closed her eyes. In spite of the kids' game play and TV noise, her weary eyes stayed shut. An hour later, she woke up and said, "I'm going to bed, guys. Good night." She got up and peeked into the girls' room. Empty.

"Where's Manda?" she asked the siblings. They looked at each other and shrugged.

Mom ran into her room, "Joe, have you seen Manda?"

Dad looked up from the paper. "No, why?"

The phone rang. Dad picked up, "Hello?"

"This is Peter Davies from Denver International Airport Security. Is this Mr. Joe Barker?"

'Y-yes," Dad said. His heart slammed in his chest.

"I have your daughter Manda here."

"What?"

"It seems she flew here, but we don't know how. She's very upset, and the only thing she'll say is that she's a ghost."

After Manda reached home, years of pain bled out from her deep wounds. Mom, Dad, and Manda met with Mrs. Compton at Portland Family Counseling Center.

Manda felt sad when she saw the hurt on her parents' faces.

Mrs. Compton helped her talk about her years of pain and why she felt as if no one ever saw her or cared about her.

Her mom and dad said that they loved their large brood but didn't have time to be alone with each one of them every day. They said that since Manda was such a quiet, easy kid, and did well in school, she got lost in the mix.

The more they talked and Manda's mom and dad came to see how she had felt for a long time, the more her hurt began to fade away. Mrs. Compton coaxed Manda to tell them more about the day she ran away and her plea to God.

She asked Manda if she thought God heard her pray. "Yes!" she said, "I didn't know if He was real, but He kept me safe and got me home." Her mother said that if Manda had gone out on the streets, it could have turned out very bad. Her father added that he thanked God every day that Manda was home safe.

After a few weeks with Mrs. Compton, the family found a church and learned more about God. Manda joined the youth group along with her brothers and sisters. She began to feel that in her family was a good place to be. They talked to each other, and her parents acted on a new plan to take each child out alone once a month. Manda began to see that her family loved her, and her very soul began to heal.

Manda had made a plea for help from a God she couldn't see and had barely met up until the day she ran away. In that time, Manda had learned her worth, not only to her family, but to Him. A holy God, who couldn't be seen, had shown her that He not only saw her but also loved her. He had brought her to a place where she could learn that He sent His son to die to save her.

Manda knew she would never feel like a ghost again.

33

COMMUNING WITH
THE DEAD

Sharon Cook

W hat's there to see?" I asked. Our cruise ship had stopped in Palermo, Italy, for the day. Norm saw the ad for the Capuchin Catacombs. He has an odd sense of what is fun and told us, "I want to see dead bodies." We looked at the map. Three miles? We can do it!

It was hot; cars were thick on the street. We passed by men as they talked on door stoops, shops that showed off their wares and food smells that blew onto our path. Each man along the way whom we asked if we were there yet, would just flick his hand toward the street and say, "More, more!"

Three miles later, tired and full of sweat, we saw "Ingresso Catacombe" in bold print over a small door. We paid our fee and went into the cool hall that led us under the ground.

We gasped as we turned the last bend and saw row after row of stiff forms on the walls. Dressed in their own clothes, some still had hair—brows, beards, manes, fringe. Some had faces that looked like faces; some just had holes for eyes, nose, and mouth. Some were on beds; some were hooked to the walls with ropes or chains.

We learned that in 1597 the monks had to have more room for their dead, so they made a new place in some caves. When it was all done in 1599, they moved some of the dead from the old place into the new one. They were stunned when later they found that the forms did not rot. It was a like a dream! One of them, Fra

Silvestro da Gubbio, can still be seen in his brown robe and in his hand a sign that bore the date, 16 Octobre 1599. His face is just a skull, and he is held up with a lot of ropes, but he's still there.

After they found how "fresh" the first set seemed, they made a way to keep others more or less whole. They drained each corpse of brains, lungs, etc., and in each now-empty place put straw or bay leaves. Placed on a grid in a dry room, each body drained for a year. At the end of the year, they were washed and dressed with their own clothes. The skin was hard and the body stiff, so it could be hung on the wall.

Each aisle has been set aside for one type. One aisle is for monks, one for priests in their rich robes, one for women in their rich robes, and one for well-known men. Each type of job has its own aisle.

By 1783, any one in the town could ask to be put there, any sex, any age. Even though it closed in 1880, two more were put there after that: Giovanni Paterniti, Vice-Consul of the United States in 1911 and two-year-old Rosalia Lombardo in 1920. We can view her in a glass case — her eyes closed, a bow in her hair, and her dress fluffed around her face. She looks as if she has just passed away

On the long walk to the ship, we talked about what we saw and how odd and weird it was. And for days, Norm would tell each one he met, "I saw dead bodies!"

34

CHILLS

E.V. Sparrow

Under the sun atop a soft grass hill, Eva sat on a warm and cozy towel with her friend, Kim, and rubbed the chill bumps on her arms.

Kim gazed at the clear view of their four kids in the park. She turned to Eva, "You're cold?"

"No, just chills." Eva spied the girls, Shay and Riley, in the fenced-in sand area. Her son, Ben, rode his red bike on the bike path. He raced past the chain-link fence as fast as his four-year-old legs could pedal. His friend, Josh, kept up with him.

Two other moms with three kids sat at the far side of the park, near the school. A young man lay sprawled out in the shade of a large elm tree and read his book.

The spring breeze blew Shay's sweet voice over to Eva. Then she heard a motor.

Two men in a beat-up beige truck cruised the length of the school's big lot. They parked away from the other four cars. Their truck had no plate.

The hairs on Eva's neck raised up. *That's odd, she thought,* as she pulled her knees to her chest.

Shay squealed.

"The girls got sand all over their dolls. It's in their hair." Kim laughed.

"They sure have fun." Eva put her chin in her hand and eyed the men. More chills ran along her neck. *Why do I have chills?* She felt God prompt her to step up her watch on the kids. *What's there to be scared of?* Eva saw her son, Ben, chase Josh by the bike path.

"I love the fenced-in area for the sand and swings. It makes me feel safe here," Kim said and sighed, "Eva? Hello, Eva? What's wrong?"

The men sat still in their truck.

"I don't know," Eva rasped. "Those men seem a bit weird."

Kim turned her head and pulled down her visor, "You mean, *those* men?"

"Let's watch them. I don't trust them." *Why are they here? We're just kids and moms.*

The man who drove the truck had a gray beard and wore a tan shirt and pants. He climbed out and walked alone fifty yards down the lot to the men's room.

"Look at that. Why would he park over here, by us, and not over by the men's restroom?" Eva asked.

"Yea, that is weird." Kim frowned. "It's a long walk."

Tan Man came out and strolled to the end of the lot.

"*Hmm.*" Eva fixed her gaze on him in time to see him head into the tall grass along the creek. It split the park and play area from the school grounds.

"Can you see him, Eva? I lost track of him."

"He's down by the creek, now." Eva raised up on her knees. Even from the top of the hill, it was hard to see him.

Tan Man climbed up the steep bank and stopped. He faced the park. He was about forty yards out.

"He's over there," Eva said.

Tan Man slid back down the creek bank and out of sight.

The kids are in the sun, while Tan Man creeps in the shade. Eva's scalp crawled as she scanned the bank for him. "I don't like how he acts."

"You watch him, and I'll watch the kids." Kim rose to her knees. "The girls are still in the fenced-in sand area."

Eva searched for the boys. "The boys are on the bike path on the far side of the fence. There's that creep, back there again. I guess he didn't find what he wanted by the creek."

Tan Man spoke to Book Man under the tree and waved his arm at the park and sand area.

Book Man looked up, shook his head, and went back to his book.

Eva glanced at Kim, "What do you think he asked that guy?"

Kim shrugged. "Maybe he lost his dog and asked if he'd seen it?"

"I hope you're right. Oh no! Where did he go? Maybe under that bridge?" Eva began to point. "He could hide there."

"What? Why would he hide?" Kim touched Eva's arm, "Here comes Ben and Josh on their bikes."

Every nerve in Eva's being tensed. "We need to get the boys."

Ben passed Josh at the turn and drew next to the bridge. Josh slowed his pace and fell back about ten feet.

Tan Man sprang out from under the bridge. He ran full speed at Ben's back. Tan Man's face held the focus of a starved lion as it stalked its prey. And his prey was Eva's son.

The scene lagged, and time froze as thoughts crashed through Eva's mind: *He's after my boy! I can't get to him!* Her heart beat fast. She couldn't breathe. She rushed to her feet.

Ben didn't see Tan Man.

Eva found her voice, "No!" Ice cold fear swept through her body. She screamed, "Ben! Come! Now!" Ben's sweet baby face flashed in Eva's mind. The feel of his hugs. *God, help us!*

Kim yelled, "Josh!"

Panic and rage drove Eva down the hill. Her ears rang. *Go to the truck — or Ben will be gone!* She faced the truck a few feet away, ready to pounce, but kept her son locked in her sight.

Ben won his race, but in the grasp of Tan Man's claws he would lose more. Ben hopped off his bike and knocked it over. With a broad grin, he sped to his mom.

Tan Man tripped over the bike and froze in his tracks. His face cleared. He glared at Eva and Kim by the hill, then jumped into his truck where his friend sat. He backed up and then his tires squealed as he spun out.

Both moms tracked the truck until it turned onto the street.

Eva blinked back tears and squeezed her son. "Mama loves you so much."

Thank You, God! Thank You! Eva gulped down a sob and clapped her hands over her mouth. Her body shook. Her heart raced.

Eva whirled to check once more on her girls and began to stroke Ben's damp head. *God, You saved my son from those evil men!* With shaky hands, she let him go. *What would they have done?* She cringed and squeezed her eyes shut.

Then she glanced about to catch Josh as he grabbed Ben, and the boys began to brawl on the grass. After a time, they laughed as Josh got up and yelled. "I'll win next time!"

35

A Wreck With a Van and a Boat

Randy Swanson

It was hot and dry in Guatemala on that washed-out dirt road filled with pot holes and sharp rocks. Dust stuck to my face as sweat-formed streaks of brown mud slid down my cheeks. The ferry was slow and filled with rust from lack of care. My Volkswagen camp van was next in line to crawl up the boat ramp and cross the strait. The weight of the VW pushed the ramp into the mud bank and the hinged lip shot up in back of the rear wheels with a crack and crash of steel on steel. I groaned. The frame of the car had been crushed. Some parts of the rear of the car seemed all-but ground into dust as well. Oil dripped from the oil pan, and I thought I was done for. Any chance I could find a VW shop in Central America was slim to none. Still, I asked and asked each time I met a man on the snail's-pace drive to the next town, but, none seemed to know of a VW shop. With a heart full of hope and faith, I prayed and prayed for help in my woe.

As I passed a sharp curve in the road, I saw an orange VW bus parked by the street. I stopped and talked to its German owner who told me, "I am a master mechanic from Germany, and I train the mechanics who work on VW engines like yours. Let me crawl under your van and take a look. I might be able to help you." He knew all of the parts of my VW van by heart and made a long list of the ones I would need to fix it. He told me of a VW shop just down the road in Guatemala City.

I limped into Guatemala City where I did find a Central

American VW shop. I was sure it would take weeks to get the parts shipped from California to fix the VW. The clerk looked at my rough list of parts which my German friend had scrawled in Spanish words. He stopped in his tracks, grinned at me, and left for the back of the shop. In a short time, he came back — his arms filled with a load of car parts. He plopped the parts on the work bench; they made quite a heap. He said, "Here you go!" I just stared at the stack as my jaw dropped.

"Where did you get all of these car parts?" I gasped with shock in my voice and also on my face.

"Well," he said. "Five months ago, a man came in to buy a list of parts identical to yours. He paid a small deposit, so I ordered the parts, and they arrived about a month ago. I have been calling and calling to reach him, but he is nowhere to be found. He just disappeared. I was getting ready to return the parts to the United States."

In the pile of parts stacked on the bench were all of the things on my list so the van was fixed, and soon I was on my way. I guess the van of some other poor fool had been crushed in the same way mine was. Or maybe the angel Gabriel, or one like him, had paid a call to help me in my time of angst and dread. I may never know for sure.

36

THE LIE

Tabitha Abel

My sister Rebecca and I left high school to start what was called our under-grad study, only she didn't have to study and I should have — but didn't. Our Mum knew Rebecca was very bright and that her smarts were like the lift that went to the top of the tower and stayed there, and I was more like the tag-along dunce whose brain made it half way to the top — and died. Rebecca bore my folly well (most of the time) but would say with a laugh, "You're such a twerp, Tabitha!" That made me feel good, even though it wasn't praise.

"What do you think of him?" I asked Rebecca about our friend, Gordon, as we rode the train home at Christmas.

"He looks a bit odd," she said — and she was right — "but he's nice. A good chap."

I had to know the truth about Gordon, but I wasn't quite sure how to put it.

"Rebecca," I said, "I don't think Gordon could have been found in a trash can. Do you? He's too smart and funny. Surely Mum was lying?"

Our Mum was known to talk straight — to the point of being rude. "Never lie, girls," she told us — and we didn't. She was as blunt as a hedge post and made us cringe, or blush, often. Why else tell Aunt Joy that cousin Tim had a nose like a rhino — even if it was true? And how come she would tell Mrs. Collins that her hot-cross buns were hot-rock buns — to her face, at the pot-luck, at church, at Easter? And worse.

We had first heard the crazy story when we were kids, but now that we had met the adult Gordon, I felt that we had make sure we had the facts right. So, I said, "Mum, you did say Gordon's mum found him in a trash can, didn't you? We've met him, and he's so nice and fun. I don't think you're right."

Her eyes flashed. She said it was true. She didn't lie, and what's more, nor did Rosemary, my big sister, To prove it, she told me I should ask Gordon, that he wouldn't mind.

"Why don't you trust me?" she said. "He'll tell you just what I said."

I knew I had to drop the topic. I was in murky water.

Rosemary was my very big sister – well, very old and not so big (or at least tall) sister. She was, and still is, 20 years older than I and a very sweet soul. She wouldn't lie. *If* she had told the story first, then I was sure he'd been found in a trash can. It must be true.

Even so, how well he's turned out! I thought.

After Christmas, when I next saw Gordon, I said nought about it. He was on top of his game and would marry Beryl in a few months. So I sent it all to the back of my empty brain where it sat for 20-years.

Four years after my query about Gordon, Rebecca had been named her class chair, and I had dropped out. "Wise choice," friends said. Rebecca made a great speech to hundreds which brought huge cheers. I was so proud of her. But that was all swept away four months later when she was hit and killed by a drunk at the wheel of a fast car. It was a huge shock, and I still miss her more than 40-years later. But every now and then I would think, *Did she never know the truth about Gordon, or did she know the real truth and never get to tell me?*

Gordon and Beryl had two sons, and I had two also and then a girl. We saw Gordon and Beryl from time to time. He still had his quirks. He joked a lot and was a great dad. He sure was a fun guy. My Mum died later of old age, and Rosemary came for the wake. For sure it would be less crazy with Mum gone.

When it was over I said to Rosemary, "I saw Gordon and Beryl two weeks ago. You know, I never was sure if Mum told me the truth when she said that Gordon was found in a trash can."

"What?" my short, older sister yelled. "What did you say?"

"Mum said Gordon was found in a trash can when he was a baby, and his Mum and Dad did all the paper work so that he's been their son all his life."

This was too much for Rosemary.

"That is so not what went on, Tabitha," she said. "Mum is a big fat liar — God rest her soul. What I told her was that when I was Gordon's third grade tutor, I said I would put him in a trash can and put the lid on it if he didn't sit down and do his work!"

"No way!" I said. "I've had pity on him for such a bad start to life, and it is a load of hooey. That can't be true. Did Rebecca know the real truth?"

"Not if she heard it from Mum."

"But, you know Mum, Rosemary. She told the truth — to a fault. I think you're lying."

It didn't go well. I should have used the few brain cells I had and kept my mouth shut. Now I would never get to the end of the story.

Today Gordon lives half a world away, on the right side of the Pond, but I see him on Facebook. Last month he was in Paris, half-way up the Eiffel Tower with Beryl.

I will never get to the truth, I thought. Now that Gordon is in his early 70s, I can't Facebook him and write, "Oh, BTW Gordon, were you found in a trash can when you were a baby?"

If he said "no" I wouldn't want him to know that I was so dumb as to think it was true. And if he said "yes," I would think he was up to his old tricks again. I guess I will go to *my* grave, never sure if he was — or wasn't — found in a trash can. What a pity! It could make such a good story.

37

A FISH TALE

Nicey Eller

If you drove by *Amber's*, home of the best key lime cake on Earth, the day I got to add *MFA* after my name, you might have seen me. I was easy to spot, in my cap and gown, on my way to find a seat. Two things were on my mind: food and roses.

I was ready for a "Kismet Scone" — a sugar shell under a fresh fruit sauce and cream — that makes taste buds dance for joy. The heart of each scone is a nest that holds a paper note, a slip of fun sure to get a smile with its hints and tips for life, a nod from Fate, or a wink from Lady Luck.

As eager as I was for a sweet treat, I was more eager to give the roses I held in my arms to an angel named Mildred.

Mildred and I hadn't seen each other since we'd met two years prior, but her faith that day we met gave my faith a boost that had kept me going ever since then. Her zest for life made me find the joy of "to" and I went to *Amber's* to thank her.

I had sat alone the day we met, ready to give up on a dream. At the small table by the door, I drank my tea and read the words typed on the crisp slip of paper that had come from my lemon scone: "Trust the fish to lead the way."

For weeks I had hoped for a sign to show me if I should go back to Lexington University, if I should sign my name on the forms in front of me so I could begin class. "Trust the fish to lead the way." So my fate had to rise or fall on fins? How could a fish speak to me?

Weary, I shut my eyes, bowed my head over my soup, and again asked God to show me what to do.

With "Amen" just off my lips, I felt a light touch on my elbow. My gaze went to the right. and there she stood. She asked if she could park her tush at my table to wait for her order, her voice as sweet and smooth as the icing on the cake I was going to take home. I couldn't stop my laugh when I saw her smile and her sassy Elvis scarf.

She held out her hand to shake mine. "By the way," she told me, "my name is Mildred. This is my Friday place for lunch!"

As she took her seat, I slid my glass over to make room for hers and slipped my fish note into my purse. When I tried to scoop up the forms in front of me, she put her hand on mine to stop me. She saw the Lexington crest on them and told me I would love being there.

I think I took too long to agree with her. She asked if the forms were for me or one of my kids. I told her they were for me, but I wasn't sure if I would go.

"If you can, you should go!" She said that like a toast, with a tap of her glass on mine. She was so sure. My eyes held hers, but they also took in her ears, each wrist, and the charm chain on her chest. She had no clue I was in search of a sign. I hoped for a fish charm or two on her ears or neck to lead the way to Lexington, but there wasn't one.

She waved her fork like a baton as she told me to sign my name right then and there, to be ready for what was to come.

I didn't look at her for fear I would cry. I didn't want to scare her or let her see just how timid I was. And I didn't want her to think being there with me was awful. Beads of sweat from my glass eased onto the table, and I kept my focus there. I told her I didn't know if I could deal with going back to class, back to hours spent with my nose and eyes in thick books, back to reams of notes, back to the stress of tests, and back to time not being my own.

She moved close to me and told me that the key to the best life was to avoid going *back*. "Just move '*to*," she said. "Leave what is past where it is. Move to what is new. Move *to*."

She cut her eyes to the left, then right, eased her chin up and said, "The only *back to* we need care about is when Jesus will come *back to* get us. Focus on what is ahead!"

Shock must have shown in my face when she said that! She told me she had seen me pray so she felt that she could say what she did about Jesus. When I let out a laugh about that, my fork fell to the floor.

But I made it fall. I'm not proud of this, but when I bent to pick it up, I aimed to see if she had a fish of any kind or even "Charlie the Tuna" inked on an ankle or foot. I was hung up on a sign to tell me to go. What she said next put an end to that quest and put peace in my heart.

"Oh, Sugar, take it from a lady who has lived a very long time. Go! Do what is in your heart. God has put that dream there. He will help you make it come true. If you want Him to bless your steps, move your feet!"

As I left, she gave me a wink, and I gave her a hug. I knew then that a sign wasn't going to let me know what to do. My heart would. God would.

"*To*" was my focus from that point on. I went to sign up for class. I read books, took notes, aced tests, and kept my mind on "to." I took all the bumps life gave me over the next two years, and I didn't look back.

Two years after we met, I went back to *Amber's* to see Mildred and to thank her for what she gave me over soup, salad, and a scone. Her smile gave me light; her words gave me hope, and her sass never left me.

Amber was busy with the lunch crowd, but she knew why I was there. The table by the door didn't have empty seats so I sat in the back area. I heard Amber tell Cicely, the girl with my tea, to keep an eye out for Mildred.

"Here you go!" Cicely said as she set my drink down. "And I'll let you know if I see Mrs. Bass come up. Isn't she a doll?"

My heart went still. Then it felt like a drum corps had taken over my chest and pulse. I kept my voice calm. "Oh, no," I said, to be sure she knew who was going to sit with me. "I'm waiting for Mildred."

"I know," she said with a smile. "Amber told me — Mrs. Mildred Bass." Her eyes lit up when she saw the door open. "Why, there she is right now!"

Mrs. Bass — Mildred — and I laugh about how we became friends. I know it sounds like a total fish tale, but it's the truth. If you eat lunch at *Amber's* any Friday, look for us at the table by the door. Feel free to join us!

38

THE THIN PLACE

Patricia Huey

That clear, crisp January day north of Seattle was quite cold. A rare azure sky and bright sun bid us join them, so Jack and I donned warm coats, hats, and boots and trekked out through the field, over the bridge and onto the dike — our first walk since we'd lost our Lab just a week prior.

We faced west, and I quipped, "Did you ever see the Olympics shine like that before? Look how close they seem!" Jack and I stared in awe.

Jack seemed taken aback. "No, I can't say I ever viewed the range like that from here, Kelly." Jack was known for his open mind, but he seemed at a loss as the peaks loomed near.

"Must be the angle of the sun. Well, it's odd, but let's go! What a day! And we can spend all of it."

Even though it was cold and our hearts sad due to our loss, we yearned to get back to the norm. A usual walk would mean that Logan was with us. A black streak ever ahead, he'd trot here and dash there, and we'd laugh at his silly romps. We missed him, our Lab of twelve years, but we had pledged to get back to our daily hikes.

As we turned from our bird's-eye view of the mount and back to the trail, I prayed that God would grant us grace. We had no child, so our dog had filled the gap. Now he was gone.

"It's called the Thin Place." At the words, Jack and I jerked back. A small man we'd met on other walks seemed to spring out of thin air.

"My goodness, Dylan! Where did you come from?" I asked,

stunned that not Jack nor I had spied him. While he was a short guy, his girth made up for it. His red hair shone in the sun. "What is a 'thin place,' by the way?" I smiled down at him. I liked him very much.

"Well, that's what we Irish call it, you know." We walked along the path as he talked. He spoke with what seemed a fake brogue, and it was all I could do not to roll my eyes.

"That's it?" I teased. "Just an Irish term?"

"It's a rare day when you see things you might not see. The Thin Place jolts us out of our old ways; it urges us to open our eyes. It's where Heaven and Earth meet, and we peer into the other realm."

The thought thrilled me. I'd felt Dillon was a bit odd in a good way, but now he'd proved it. I reached for Jack's gloved hand. He looked at me and winked which said, "Let's go along with it."

But the truth was that the peaks in the west seemed to grow ever large as we stood there. A grand sight.

About then, we strolled up to a Y in the path. Dillon waved and went one way while we traipsed out toward the far woods with the now-giant Olympic range ahead. For many years, Logan had loved this walk.

"See ya, Dillon!" I shouted.

"Open your eyes, Lass. It's a rare day!" he teased.

"Odd man," Jack laughed, a zip in his step.

Our eyes, not used to the sun, tried to focus. As we passed the "seal hole" where seals from the Sound liked to swim, I saw a bright flash. It came from the edge of the woods where the trees that lined each side of the path bowed to each other and formed a dome. A quaint place.

"What on earth was that?"

"I'm not sure."

And then he came into view. His teal-blue eyes shone in the light; his pale, grey fur flashed again in the sun. He looked part wolf, part Lab. His thick coat masked his age. Charmed, I called to him, but he made a regal turn and walked onto the domed path. Of course we went with him into the woods. What else could we do?

The wolf-dog seemed to lure us on as if under a spell. I hoped he had a home. A few lucky folks lived by the river not far off, so maybe he lived there in a warm cabin.

Jack and I both stood mute, so rapt were we. At times we lost sight of the dog, but then we'd see the light-streak. He would stop and look at us, then peer ahead. We trailed him, spell-bound, deep into the woods, — a place we had not been, at least up to this time. At last we came to a wide spot. The wolf-dog was gone.

"Where on Earth did he go, Jack?" My breath came in gasps. Jack seemed to pant, as well.

"I don't know, Kel, but I'm not sure we need to walk on. I'm cold, and I bet you are, too."

I thought the dog had moved ahead of us. But when I squinched my eyes, I found him in back of us! We turned to head back, but he blocked our way. Those eyes. Clear and bright as ice. Keen with a sharp gaze. They touched my soul. I fell into them. For the first time in days, I felt joy in the midst of calm. He turned his fine head to where the sun shone on a path through some vines, and off he dashed.

"This is too much, Kel! Let's head back." I could tell that Jack meant it.

"Oh, come on, please!" We walked down the small path, and I was glad we did. We stood there, gripped by a grand front-row view of the Olympics peaks above. Up by a cliff, I thought I spied birds, but no! Were those folks up there? I peered at them. The color was so vivid and a lush scent fell upon us from above.

"Look, Kel!" I followed Jack's gaze. A black Lab climbed from the cliff and onto a ridge. As he drew near, I could make out a white patch on his chest. This dog was a clone of our well-loved Logan, only this dog was young. He seemed happy to see us. The dog looked straight at us, and I could swear he smiled at us.

Must be owned by the folks on the cliff, I guessed.

Our old, gray wolf guide raced up to the ridge and perched next to the Lab. They seemed like old friends.

"I'm fine, you know!"

"What? Who said that?" I looked at Jack. He had heard it, too. Jack shook his head.

"It sounded like it came from the ridge, didn't it? It wasn't the wind, and we know it can't be the dog!"

"We do?" Jack spoke in a hushed tone.

The cold turned to warmth. I looked at Jack, and he hugged me. We turned to walk back home, but the gray one was gone. In his place was a red leash. I picked it up. Etched on it was one word: "Logan." We had lost that leash some time ago. For a bit, we were both lost in thought. I was not yet able to put all this in order in my mind, so it was time to go home.

On the way back, we once again ran into Dillon who said, "Hey, you two look like you've seen a ghost!" We told him what had happened. "Oh, you saw him — the old gray one with the eery blue eyes? Only a few have seen him, you know. Some say he comes out only on bright days with azure skies. Rare days. Today he's out since it's a Thin Place, don't you see? What did he show you?"

"A glimpse of an old friend," I said and walked away. Jack joined me.

"He gave you a glimpse into Heaven, didn't he?" Dillon was not one to let things go.

"Yes, he did, Dillon." I clutched the leash and turned to wave, but Dillon was gone. I looked at Jack, who shrugged.

"Let's go home, Kel," Jack urged.

"Yes, let's."

The Olympics seemed back to their usual size now. We walked over the bridge and through the field with heart-felt joy. Our grief over a black dog with a white patch on his chest had been healed.

39

THE DAIRY QUEENS'
SWEET REVENGE

Kenneth Avon White

When you're from a big city it's easy to think you've heard it all. That was my case when I moved from Dallas to Marble Falls, Texas, to take on a new job with less stress. My chance brush with a news hound from the local paper, *The Highlander*, changed all that. It was my first Saturday in town, and if I did not find a great cup-of-joe I was going to crawl out of my skin. I hit up the Blue Bonnet Café on word of mouth. Wardy Hogg. That's the name of the news guy. Son of Ima Hogg who was the daughter of former Governor Hogg. No joke. He was quick to let me know that just because I was "city folk" I had *not* heard all there was to hear. To make his point, this shell of a man (my guess from a mix of age, booze, and too many smokes) told me an odd story.

It had all begun with "The Teachers" of Marble Falls High School, dubbed so by the school's kids due to the group's mafia-esque bond — that "Ya Ya and the Sister of the hood stuff." They had set on a series of Friday after-school treks to the Dairy Queen on Ranch Road. It was their place to vent about this or that rebel pupil and Principle Thomas, the new top dog who would morph into an ogre when one-on-one with any of them. He liked to hunt down faults and add to their work load. Most thought that he planned to hire a whole new young bunch in their stead. (Many of The Teachers were up in years.)

Wardy took out a piece of creased old news print tucked away next to his money and credit cards. "Here's a picture of The Teachers," he said. "Long 'bout Christmas that first year, they had had it up to here with Thomas." As Wardy said this, he made a very slow and eerie move with his hand to slice the air from left to right over his head. One Friday at the Dairy Queen, they all made a pact. It was time go. On Monday, one-by-one they shared with Thomas their plans to exit by the end of the school year. Shelby Graham, who taught math, went first. Then Kandi Enright, who taught drama. Kandi owns this café. Then the rest."

"You don't say," I said, as I sipped.

"Ya know what's funny 'bout the whole dang thang?"

"Let me guess, making plans for such a big step nose-deep into an ice cream cone?"

"Heck no! Dairy Queen made The Teachers our town stars." I sipped on, with my brain only half in tune to his words.

"So, Kandi tells me when I spoke to her for my news story that at their Dairy Queen vent fest that Friday, they also agreed they had to go out with a bang. As the gods of Texas would have it, a lady who was sitting next to 'em said, 'If that Thomas guy has put you down so much, I know just how to get even. Enter to win the right to build Dairy Queen's Memorial Day Parade float and ride it down Main Street as their guests of honor!' With that she pulled out a flyer with all the rules."

"So what'd they do?" I asked.

"They took a shot at it. But Thomas tried to fowl things up. To vote on the best float scheme, folks had to write their name on a piece of paper and drop it off at Dairy Queen. To push The Teachers over the top, those Marble Falls High kids held a rally at school and got each squirt to sign a piece of paper or two…sometimes three. The Cheer Team. The sport teams. The Math Club. You name it. They all came. The Teachers too! When Thomas heard of it, He put a stop to that rally. 'We can't show favor on school grounds,' he said. Then Mrs. Graham piped up with, 'To the DMV lot!' The whole mob took their trash cans full of names, pens, and paper and stormed the Texas Department of Vehicles car lot next to the school where they just kept goin'."

"What did Thomas do?"

"What could he do?"

"Did they win?"I asked, now fully hooked.

Wardy sighed. "They did, but it was a close call."

"Do tell."

"The Teachers didn't think it through. When the man said, 'How ya gonna get 'er built?' there's not a peep from any one of 'em. 'know why?"

"Cat got their tongues?"

"They didn't have a plan to build it! And it waaasss biiiiig. Wanna know how big?"

"You got me hooked. Reel it in."

"The Teachers set out to glide down Main Street on top of a forty-foot Dairy Queen Lady Bird Banana Split.

"President Johnson's Lady Bird?"

"Darn right. Dairy Queen puts these candy bits of blooms on top of each scoop. Lady Bird was big on things that bloom."

At that point, Wardy's eyes got *huge*. "Well there she is, in bright lights!" I turned to see a tall woman with snow-white hair pulled back into a long, sleek pony tail. Black tights hugged her thin legs, and her long torso hid in a bright red baggy shirt with beads that glowed in the light. Draped over her arms was a multi-foot tie-dyed scarf that stretched across her back and bore the words, "I *am* about the biz of show."

Wardy sprung to life. "He-llooo drama mama!"

"Well hey back atcha," she said as she began to strut toward us over the worn vinyl floor of her café.

"I'd like you to meet Kandi Enright," Wardy said. "She can pick up the story from here on. Ask her what you asked me."

"Nice to meet you." I said.

"Oh la-la!" she breathed.

"Wardy tells me The Teachers won a big Dairy Queen deal, but then you almost lost it. How's that?"

"Oh that ol' story! Who wants to hear *that*?" she teased.

"Start with Shelby's brain freeze," Wardy said.

"Hmmm. Well we won but didn't have a plan to build our idea. All we knew was that we'd need one of those long semis with an open bed big enough to put a giant Lady Bird Banana Split on. When that man asked Shelby, 'How're y'all gonna build it?' she just froze.

"All I could think was, *The show must go on!* Then it came to me. *If I can get my drama kids to help us build a stage set, we can do this thing.* So I yanked the mic from Shelby, and that's what I told the crowd.

"How'd it turn out?"

"You from Texas?"

"Yeah."

"Aaalllll thangs come big in Texas, right? Big is part of who we are, right?"

"Yeah."

"So we built a darn big Lady Bird Banana Split and put it on the back of a big truck. That's how it turned out." She grinned.

"My wood shop boys carved out candy blooms. Then they cut two long pieces of wood curved up on each end to look like two halves of a Tropicana Banana . . . with the seal and all. Those boys got their 4H friends to build our scoops of ice cream out of chicken-coop wire mesh. And my prop crew sewed white, red, and brown cloth 'round the wire coop scoops to look like ice cream. Building those scoops was tricky cuz each scoop had to seat two queens."

"Queens?"

"Heck yeah. We set out to leave school with a bang! That was the whole point. To show Principle Thomas that if his plan was to make us look small, we'd rise above it all! So, we thought since this was a Dairy Queen float, we'd ride as queens — all in ball gowns and long white gloves and each of us with a big 'ol crown.

A regal court whisked down Main Street as guests of honor."

"What was the best part for you?" I asked.

She took a short pause. "That's easy I guess. About a block into the Memorial Day Parade, we heard a voice scream out 'Dairy Queens!' Block by block more chimed in. "Dairy Queens! Hail to The Dairy Queens!' At first, I thought they were saying, 'Hell to the Dairy Queens' but Martha, who taught Home Ec set me straight.

"Why was that the best part?" I asked.

Kandi looked out the café's large glass pane onto Main Street.

"Have you ever been cheered on? You know, in the center of it all? For one year we went through hell at school. For two weeks we passed through it again with the whole design, vote, and build thing. But all of it got us to our big-bang exit. For three hours we were queens on top of the world! They clapped. They cheered. We reigned. And then there's the cherry on top of our Lady Bird Banana Split. Know what it was?"

"Can't even guess," I said.

"Principle Thomas, who had long since signed up to be a Memorial Day Parade clown, was placed next to our float and had to dance at our feet the whole way. Isn't chance the oddest thang?"

At that point, I was stumped for words.

40

BUSY IN THE NIGHT

Mary Hunt Webb

The clock by my bed said it was 2 a.m. — the time of night when most of Cheyenne, Wyoming slept. But our baby had kicked me awake. I closed my eyes, but he or she wouldn't quiet down. As strong as those kicks were, we guessed that Baby was a boy, but we didn't know for sure.

Kick, kick, kick. Sigh! How could I get back to sleep with all that going on in me!

Might as well get up, I thought. With my husband at work on the night shift, Baby and I were alone in the house that we had just bought in April. Now, in June, I was warm all the time. *Maybe some juice will cool Baby and me down at the same time.* Just a few more weeks of this and Baby would be born. Going to the fridge, I pulled out the juice and poured some into a glass.

When I turned to the sink and looked through the glass panes above it, I saw a flash of light in the street that stretched by our house. *Who would be out there at this hour?* Through the glass, I saw two men by the trunk of a car. I couldn't see who they were — thanks to the leaves of the tree under which they stood. They also faced the street so that their backs were to me. What were they doing? What was that in their hands? A bike. They had a bike that they tried to put into the trunk of the car.

As I sipped the juice, I watched the men work with the bike for a while. At last, one of them got on the bike and began to pedal away down the street while the other one got into the car and drove in the wake of the other man. What in the world was that all about?

By then, Baby was calm so that I was able to go back to bed and get some sleep.

I didn't think about it again until the next day when I was out in our yard and saw Mary, the older lady next door. She was the mother of Jeannie, aged 13, as well as of an older daughter and son.

"Did you hear about our theft last night?" she asked.

"No, I didn't."

"Some thieves took Jeannie's bike!"

"Oh, Mary!" I said. "The baby woke me up last night so that I saw two men in the street by our house." Since Mary had given birth three times, she knew what it was like to be awake with a baby. "That's when I saw them try to put a bike in the trunk of a car, but it must not have fit." After I told her the rest of what I had seen, I added, "I'm so sorry, but I didn't know what was going on!"

Mary shook her head. "You couldn't have known. At any rate," she said as she looked at my tummy, "you have a lot on your mind right now. Just a few more weeks and you will be very busy!"

41

THE BOY

He was only eight. Just a blonde-haired, blue-eyed boy with a cute turned up nose. He would grin up at his mom when he had been a bad boy and would slyly say, "You would not hit a poor wee boy would you?" She had never hit him in the past, so why he would say this would leave her stumped, but she could never be mad at such a cute little face, with that smile full of holes. Her anger would melt into a laugh, a hug, and a kiss. No, she could never stay mad at this one.

His dad, on the other hand, also loved him, but he was stern and hard on his son. He had grown up in a harsh way, so his goal was to train his boy to be tough. Every Saturday night, the dad would drive the boy to a paper stand and have the boy sell the *Post Dispatch*.

One night in the deep winter freeze, the small boy fell asleep in the back seat of the car on the way to his stand. When his father woke him, he had wet his pants. The father made him stand there, drenched pants and all, to work in the cold night air.

The boy shook as he froze in his wet pants. A guard took pity on the poor little fella and let him come into the guard shack to warm a bit, even though his pants smelled of urine. The boy went back to his post, took the coins, made change, and gave out the paper. He did his job as well as any boy who is only eight years old and icy cold.

When the job was done and he reached home, his mom gave him a warm bath and wrapped him under a cozy cover. The boy never forgot that night and the harsh way his father had dealt with him, the kind act of the guard, and the sweet touch of a mother.

The boy would later grow to be a fine man who would have a son of his own. He never held a grudge about his dad as he knew down deep that these were the things that shaped him. These were the things that made him thrive, as a father, as a husband, and as a friend. These were the things that would help him to excel in his work.

He would one day win the Nobel Peace prize. His life was built on this motto, "Some of the time life is hard and harsh, and some of the time life is sweet and soft, but there are always times to be aware of those who need your help, and it's just a nice thing to show some pity."

42

THE FIRST LIBRARY

Jacinta S. Fontenelle

The big old house could not be missed. It stood tall where Hilt and Grant streets met. Devin's friend Kelan used it to teach him the route from home and school.

"This is the home of Mrs. Rickety Rack," his new friend Kelan had told him a few weeks after his family moved to this new town. What a strange name, he thought! More so when he caught sight of the old lady who was given that name.

Devin wished that his mom had not moved them so far from his few friends. It was not easy for him to make friends and in his short seven years of life he had only three boys that he could call pals. These they had left back home when they moved here. He tried hard not to cry as he thought of how sad he felt and how much he missed his friends.

The sound of Mrs. Rickety's name brought him back from his sad thoughts. Kelan told him how nice she was. The name made him think of a small lean-to that was old and worn.

Kelan was the first friend he had made here so far. He was kind and made sure to help him find his way in the new school. Kelan was well liked, but he did not seem to care that Devin was shy. Kelan seemed glad to take Devin to meet Mrs. Rickety but would not tell him any more about her name.

On that day, the teachers had a half-day conference, so they got to leave school after lunch. Three of them were walking home when Devin heard Kelan shout, "There is Mrs. Rickety." They all turned to where he pointed and there, about to cross the street was a short, small old lady dressed in bright red. Kelan waved, and her face seem to light up when she saw them. She turned and crossed over to them, with a warm smile. As she drew near, Devin saw that she had a gleam in her eyes, as if she had a thought that brought her joy. Kelan walked over to Mrs. Rickety and told her why they were out of school this early. Devin turned when Kelan called his name. "Waaht?" he asked, as the two boys joined them. Kelan saw to it that Mrs. Rickety met Devin and the other boy, Hober, who seemed even more shy than Devin.

"Mrs. Rickety has asked us to visit her big old house," Kelan said. "She says we can call our parents from her house. Her grandchildren are at the house, and that way we can meet them."

Even though he had just met her, Devin was glad, for he felt happy near Mrs. Rickety. Hober had a rare smile on his face as he looked at Mrs. Rickety. She was an old lady, warm and friendly, with a smile that made you feel good all over. But still, Devin could not see why she was called by that name.

Since they were only a block and a half from her home, she had them hold hands with her and set off. The big old house looked huge from the outside, but as they went in the large front room he felt as if he had crossed over into a changed world. As far as the eyes could see were books — on the floor-to-ceiling shelves, on the tops of tables, on racks near big plush chairs which could hold more than one small guy like him. On the floor was a bright rug made up of blue, gold, green and red fluffy squares with a small pile of books on each square.

On each of three of the squares, he saw a child about his age — faces buried in a book. Mrs. Rickety took the three boys over to the phone on a small table and told them to first call their parents to let them know where they were. As Devin waited his turn, he felt as if he should pinch himself. *Was this a dream?*

He was sure his eyes were as big as the moon and his mouth gaped open, but he didn't care; he was just stunned at this place and knew that it was unlike any other in the whole world. On the shelves of books, he could also see pictures of strange animals he did not know as well as some pets that he could only dream of.

On a small round table close by, he saw one of the books he liked best; a pop-up book of animals. He felt as if the pages drew him in, but he came back to the sound of Mrs. Rickety as she said, "Your turn, Devin." He breathed a sigh of thanks that his mom had met Mrs. Rickety, and once she heard that he was with Kelan she said yes. He barely heard her tell him the time to be home for their meal and with a, 'Bye Mom' hung up the phone. *Now for the fun* he thought to himself.

"I call this room, Ms. Lib's Sanctuary. These are my grand-daughters Libbie and Angil and my grandson Kandun," Mrs. Rickety said with a look of love as she turned to the kids. "Come meet some new friends," she called to the three grandchildren. They were slow to turn from their books, but with warm smiles — which seemed to be a family trait —came over to meet the new friends. Hober did not seem at all shy and was soon on the green square with Angil, in his hand the book she had given him.

Devin was pulled to one side by Kandun who, it seemed, had seen the way he looked at the pop-up book and took him to see the shelf where the set of pop-up books were kept.

Mrs. Rickety Rack said, "My friends and their friends are meant to find joy here, but first a few rules. No food in this room; no loud noises —indoor voices only." She then went on to show what that type voice should sound like. "Take care of the books; they are your friends. They will take you to new and wonderful places and teach you many new things. Share and be kind. Now, have fun as I leave you with my friend Joyline while I take care of some chores."

That's when Devin saw that there was a young lady in the room. As Mrs. Rickety and the boys looked at her, she glanced up and smiled. She waved her hand with a calm word of welcome on her lips.

This was the first of quite a few great times in Ms. Lib's Sanctuary. With the help of Ms. Joyline, Devin soon found other types of books that he liked — books on horses, dogs, cats, and other pets that he had not heard of, like pigs. He saw all kinds of books. When he asked Ms. Joyline or Mrs. Rickety a question they made him feel smart, for Mrs. Rickety often said that the most stupid question is the one that has not been asked.

The three friends asked their parents to do their homework at Ms. Rickety's and raced there right after school. They would have loved to rush through their homework to get to the books but not under Ms. Joyline's watch. She helped them if they needed, but no books were allowed until their homework was all done.

Mrs. Rickety's grandchildren seemed to love Ms. Lib's Sanctuary as much as the three boys, and even though they lived an hour away they came over every time they were out of school. Once in a while their parents came too and seemed to love Ms. Lib's Sanctuary just as much. The boys and Mrs. Ricketty's grandchildren were soon best friends. It was not long before Devin, Kelan, and Hober were the top students in their class.

That first Christmas, Devin knew he wanted to give Mrs. Rickety a gift that told of his thanks for Ms. Lib's Sanctuary, which meant so much to him. In art class he learned to make cards and when the teacher said they could write poems or a note he wrote Mrs. Rickety a poem.

Mrs. Rickety Rack
She has our back.
She keeps us on track
And helps us make the mark
In Ms. Lib' sanctuary
Our very first Library.

His friends liked the poem so they all signed it and gave it to Mrs. Rickety Rack. It was a Christmas he would never forget, for he learned the story behind the names, Mrs. Rickety Rack and Ms. Libs Sanctuary. On this Christmas they all came up with the best gift for her birthday on New Year's day — a blue, gold, green, and red sign that read, "Our Very First Library." Mrs. Rickety Rack was proud to put the sign on the door to Ms. Lib's Sanctuary.

42

A MONTH OF GOOD DEEDS

Kelly Pankratz

I peered from my tent to take in the sun's hues as it rose above the Bitterroot Mountains in the Idaho Panhandle. The past two days had pleased us more than we'd hoped. Today, we'd set out for a four-hour bike ride up the mount to cruise the fun path down to the stream near the base. I'd longed to meet God on this trip, and He did not hedge.

As Greg and I crossed the crest, though, we eyed huge rocks and downed trees. Should we bail and find a safer route? The map showed an easy road. We knew it would clear soon and each pushed our cycle over rocks and stumps. A half hour. An hour. Six hours. The jaunt should have been done, but we could see no soon end to the trip.

The day's heat pressed down as we sat under a large tree and sucked the last from our flasks.

"We should turn back," Greg rasped.

He might have been right, but I couldn't quit. "We can do it. The path will smooth out soon. It has to." We could see no road-closed sign; plus, I'd planned this trek. I had to get Greg to the win.

A stir in the woods pricked my skin. Greg slapped my arm as I looked to our right to see a large moose step from the brush and begin to stare us down. He could charge and end us in no time. Greg clutched the gun at his side. I prayed. After a long stare, the beast gave a snort, looked to his left, and marched into the woods. We both let out pent-up breaths, and I crashed back to the earth. God had moved the moose. He would move us. "Let's go, before it gets dark."

We pushed on, over crags, around downed wood. Our hands ached at the weight of our bikes. My brain mocked the land. You can't take me down.

As dusk fell, we knew we had to make camp. We drank from a creek, slept on rock, and prayed a bear wouldn't dine on us for a late meal. After sparse sleep, I woke with the birds. I snacked on dried fruit and nuts and gauged our odds on a way out. We couldn't turn back. No way to get the bikes up that trail. Greg stirred, and I nudged him. "C'mon. I want to get out of here." My phone had died the day prior but had no cell bars even when it had power. Greg had brought a Sat phone in case the need arose. I hoped it wouldn't.

We packed camp and trudged ahead. The sun beat on our backs. Our gear hung like bricks on tired bones. With each rock and downed tree, we cursed the wild woods. As a team, we would take gear off a bike, push it over each snag, go back for the gear, then do the same with the other bike. After four hours, we had gone half a mile.

We found a spot in the shade for a rest. Flat on the ground, Greg sighed. "We should walk out. Leave the bikes."

I looked at my hands. Cuts and bruises tore my skin. Blood streaked to each wrist. "No. We can do this." I knew he didn't agree. I wasn't even sure that I thought it was true, but I couldn't find the will to give up. Not yet.

"We can't quit."

Greg sat and stared into my eyes. "Then let's move."

We grabbed our bikes and inched down the hill. My body ached, and I begged my trained mind to offer strength. I brought the cycle along and up a huge rock, then over and down. As my boot slipped on shale, I lost hold and dropped. The cycle crashed and pinned me to the earth. With my leg wedged beneath the weight of the bike, every nerve in my body screamed.

"Greg." I winced. "Help."

Greg stood above me, like a giant. He gaped and heaved for

breath. "I can't. I have no strength. I'm sorry." He slumped to the ground.

"Don't pass out." I moaned.

"I won't."

"I don't mean you. I mean me." I laid my head back on the rock, closed my eyes, and prayed. God, help me lift this bike, and I will walk out. I'll leave it all here where no man will ever find it. Deep breath. I pulled my upper body close to the bike and shoved the metal. My arms burned in pain. Push. Nope. Push. I sensed a small shift. Push. One inch, maybe two.

"Twist your leg." Greg yelled and pulled on the bike.

I shoved one last time and yanked my leg free. Thank you, God, and thank you for armor shin guards. I was sure there'd be a bruise but felt no break. I crawled off the path and sat hunched under a tree. Tears formed and ran as I cupped my face against my knees. I knew I had to leave, or next time it could be my life. Greg plopped near me. Sober quiet. No words, but we knew it was time to yield to that which held more power than we did. A rare breeze blew through the leaves above. In my heart, the Spirit of God spoke.

Our minds were in chaos. As we threw gear from the bikes, we chose what to carry out. How far was out? I grabbed the gift I'd bought for my daughter at Glacier, my son's GoPro, my phone, and a few other items. Greg marked our spot on the Sat phone, in case we ever made it back — if we ever got out.

We hiked through trees to where I thought a road might be. After an hour, we hit flat dirt. I tore my boots off and tossed them aside. My feet breathed for the first time in two days. I flexed my toes and slipped them into thongs. The day grew long, and we had no time to waste. My best guess was we had twenty miles to a paved road. We'd have to sleep along the dirt once the dark took over. Best to go as far as we could.

As Greg and I limped, we both grew lost in our thoughts. This trip was planned to be a time to rest my soul and to face things in my life back home that I had to let go of. I hoped God would give me strength while on this trek with my best friend. Now, I walked away from more. Not just the mess at home, but my loved cycle and gear. My hobby. I knew there'd be no new bike ahead. It was over. If I made it home, I'd be blessed to have my life. Please help me to make it home.

Bright light streamed ahead. I scrunched my eyes. "Greg." I thrust my hand toward an old steel bridge with the sun's glare coming from it. We stopped and stared. "That bridge has been washed out." Greg croaked. "What kind of force can do that?"

"Earth has some fury when it wants to." I felt chilled, in spite of the heat.

"We're never gonna make it."

"Yes, we will." I nudged him as we stepped into sync again.

The dead bridge lay quiet and still as a stream flowed near. Water. Our feet moved to find the shore until I stopped dead in my tracks. Parked, on the other side of the bridge, was a shiny blue truck. We gawked, looked at each other, then gawked again.

To my side, I heard a crunch and jumped, like a caged wolf close to death. Then peace. A man and his son walked up the bank. I thought he might have been an angel. They paused when we came into their sight.

I stepped close. "We need help." I held my hands in the air.

"You look like you need help."

"We need a ride…to a town…where we can rent a car."

Greg piped in. "I have a gun, but I'll put it in the back. I won't shoot you."

The man grinned. "I didn't think you would." He threw their poles into the truck bed. "Hop in. We're Boy Scouts. It's our goal to do a good deed every day."

"This will last you a month."

43

MINISTERING ANGELS

Dottie Lovelady Rogers

The glass door swished as it slid open in front of the old man. He pulled his coat about him as he made his way to the car through the cold, damp night. All the lights in the lot were ringed by halos of mist. He was peeved to hear the sound of his own heels tap on the hard street, since no one else was out here at this wee hour. The dark began to sink into his soul as he pressed his key to open the door lock.

It feels so strange to leave her like this. I won't be back to get her. He sank into the seat and took a deep breath. It had been a long day and night. He had sat by his wife's side as she fought for her life, but she had lost her war with death. No more could be done.

He turned on the motor, fixed the heat, but could not leave. He looked back at the exit he'd just passed through. *Where is she now? Is she still in the same room? Have they moved her yet? Yes, of course. They need the space for...* He thought he should have sat with her a bit more. They said he could take his time. But he'd left. He just had to get out of there. And now he couldn't leave the grounds.

I guess she's in the morgue with the rest of those who've died. Every day folks die in there. He looked up the six stories to the roof. In his mind's eye, he could see many souls make their flight up from their sick rooms toward the sky. He was not sure what came next for them — for her. Had she been met by an angel to guide her on her way?

I've got to get home, to get some rest. He wasn't sure when he'd had his last meal, but he felt empty. He could eat some eggs and toast. *I've got so much to take care of today. Like phone calls to let folks know she's gone, and I've got to make plans for the...* Now he was mad. *She was the one who took care of all that stuff. She's dead, and they will still send me the bill. She paid the bills too. I don't know how I'm going to make it. When I get home, I'll be alone.* He turned off the motor. *I should have stayed. I shouldn't have left so soon.* He gripped the wheel, and slumped forward with guilt, but his head hit the wheel too hard. It hurt, and he rubbed the knot that came up fast.

"No, she should have stayed! She shouldn't have left so soon," he said aloud. "She was my angel." Now, for the first time, he felt hot tears come to his eyes. The warmth made his specs fog up. He took them off to wipe the wet away from his eyes and licked the salt taste from his lips. He thought, *Get a grip, man. There's time for this later.* He shook from the chill of the night and turned the car on again, but still did not put it in drive. *I don't know how I can do this alone. I wish I were dead too. Where's my angel?*

Then he thought he heard a noise. He looked to his left to see a face peer back at him. It was the night guard who had tapped on the glass. "You ok in there, Bud?"

"Yeah, I'm ok."

The guard told him to roll down the glass. "I saw that you've been out here a long time. I thought you might be sick or need help."

"No," the man said. He sniffed. He had to blow his nose, but all he saw near him was his wife's scarf in the other seat. He blew his nose on the scarf and could smell her scent on it. His heart sank.

The guard didn't let up. "Can I help? What do you need?"

"I just lost my wife." His voice was too loud and cold.

"Oh. Sorry to hear it. I lost mine a few years ago too." The guard's face was kind. The old man felt bad that his reply had been so harsh.

Still, "Hey, I just made a pot of java," the guard said. "'you want to come in and have a cup with me? Let me get you a cup. It'll warm you up."

"No, I've got to get home. I need some sleep."

"I do too. It's decaf." Then the guard took off his right glove and reached through the open space to shake hands. "My name's Michael. What's yours?"

"I'm Grady." The two men shook hands. "You said it's Michael? Like the angel?"

With a nod, Michael grinned. "Like the angel. It's been a cold night, hasn't it? Hey, are you starved? I might have some sweet rolls in there too."

Grady turned off the motor again and got out of his car. "I guess I will have a cup with you. 'feels like my life's on hold right now. I've never had to face this kind of thing. Janice…her name is Janice. She was my wife for forty-seven years."

As they walked toward the guard house, Michael seemed to know he should just be quiet and let Grady talk. The night guard was done with his shift, but his real job had just begun. As all his friends knew, his motto had always been, "You never clock out of the Lord's work."

Both men looked up to see the sun begin to glow red in the east.

44

MY MOTHER, THE SPEEDSTER

Lanita Boyd

My mother was never shy about the times she was stopped for going over the speed limit and took pride in her skill to "talk my way out of a ticket."

"Oh, officer! I am so sorry if I was too fast!" Mother would say with a sweet smile. Then she would bring forth one of her main pleas.

"I need to get my sick daddy to the doctor, and I'm late," scored a win. Over the years the words changed from "daddy" to "mama" to "neighbor" as the folks who were sick, but the end was the same. Her clear upset and the sweet way she had about her turned the man who had pulled her over into ally in her cause. He was sure to see her on her way and not hold her up. He wouldn't cite her but just would warn her and then she was off. In fact, on one stretch of road on the 20 miles from her house to her mother's, she was stopped so much by the same cop that once when he stopped her car he said, "Oh, it's you, Mrs. Bradley! Does your father have to go to the doctor again?"

When I was a teen, she was in her thirties and men were drawn to her. One plea I often heard when she had been stopped was, "My husband will be home soon, and I want to have our food ready when he gets there." She would add a coy smile and then a shy gaze that said, "Can't you imagine how nice it would be to have such a pretty wife who wants to hurry home to get *your* supper?" Again, all the poor man would do was warn her, and then we were off.

In the early years, that charm and warm smile served her well; in later years, the white hair and grandmotherly air seemed to melt the cops' hearts. The naive, "Who — me?" look she would give along with her words had its effect as well. "Now you slow down, you hear?" the man of the hour would say, and she was on her way. It was lucky for her that she was always stopped by a male officer; her charm didn't go very far with women. And all her lead-foot ways were in Tennessee, where men are known for how they defer to women.

Odd as it may seem, she kept count of how many times she'd been stopped for going too fast. On the way to my son's 18th birthday party, she was stopped for the 18th time. She thought that was quite a lark but had the common sense not to share that odd fact with the long arm of the law who had pulled her over. At the party, however, she held all under her spell as she told the story. Prior to this, she'd not been able to use "I'm late to my grandson's birthday party," but it had worked.

When, in her eighties, she reached her 25th stop, she decided that he time had come for her to pay her dues. As she drove her new car home, she had no last case left to make for going over the speed limit and didn't even try to dream one up. When the cop who had pulled her over came up, she pushed the button to lower the glass, but it didn't budge. She waved her hands in the air, then had to open the door to talk with him. "I'm sorry, officer," she said. "This is a new car and I can't seem to get the window down."

He helped her solve how to turn off the lock and lower the glass. Then he said, "Well, I can see why you were speeding, ma'am. You're just not used to this new car. I'll let you off this time, but you slow down, now, you hear?"

ABOUT THE AUTHORS

Tabitha Abel (p. 110) grew up in England and now lives in southern Oregon, on the wrong side of the Pond. She has 10 grandchildren, some her own and some from a blending of her and her husband's families. Retired from being a medical professional, she's a knitter, committed freelance writer, triathlete, outdoors woman, and amateur musician.

Much of what she says can be taken with a grain of salt these days, although her most important mission in life is to reach her family and others for God.

Despite the very rough edges of life, God sustains her and her husband Gary, through its difficulties. Tabitha blogs weekly on Facebook at Tabel Talk@TabithaBCAbel where she writes about This and That from a Christian Perspective. You can contact her at TabithaAbel@yahoo.com.

Karen O'Kelley Allen (p. 16) has a passion for music, ministry, and dogs. On Sundays she plays the organ for her church, Meadow Brook Baptist Church in Birmingham, Alabama where she and her husband of 35 years, George Parker (Parky), attend. On weekdays she works as a quality assurance manager in the area of cancer research at the University of Alabama Comprehensive Cancer Center. She enjoys spending vacations on the mission field at home and internationally.

A diagnosis of breast cancer inspired her to write her Bible study Confronting Cancer with Faith(www.confrontingcancerwithfaith.com), which has brought encouragement to people around the world. Karen enjoys speaking, singing, and writing and has published numerous articles and devotionals through LifeWay Christian Resources, Grace Publishing, and Christian magazines and newspapers such as *The Alabama Baptist*.

Joylene M. Bailey (p. 28) grew up on the Canadian prairies where rolling hills, just-mowed hay, and the meadowlark's trill make her heart sing. She will always be a prairie girl. Joy writes because what began as making up childhood stories to put herself to sleep at night, became creating stories and songs for her three daughters. This fun activity morphed into writing articles and stories for children's publications.

Since then she has written short stories, poetry, songs, and devotionals. Her current work in progress is a novel about a wandering little girl and her flawed-but-loving mother. Joy hosts a merry and productive writers group in Edmonton, Alberta, where she lives with her husband, daughter number three, and an impish cat named Calvin. She shares her joy-infused view of the world at www.scrapsofjoy.com.

Lanita Bradley Boyd (p. 139) is a freelance writer and speaker who draws on years of teaching, church ministry, and family experiences in her writing. She enjoys mentoring young women through Bible studies and planning spiritually uplifting events.

Lanita travels with her family and has been on mission trips lasting three-to-six-weeks each. On these trips to Brazil, Panama, Fiji, Malaysia, and Thailand, she offers free English lessons based on Bible stories. She also works locally to help new English speakers improve their language skills.

Lanita is married to Stephen Boyd — speaker, author, and minister. They live in Fort Thomas, Kentucky, a suburb of Cincinnati, Ohio, where they serve at the Central Church of Christ. They have a son and daughter who brought to the family another daughter and son and four wonderful grandchildren. She can be reached at lanitaboyd@gmail.com.

Jenny Calvert has always had a love for writing, but with church work and children, she had to put it on the back burner of her life. Now that she is older, and her children are raised, she has rekindled this passion.

A contributing writer for dailyprayer.us under the link Daily Inspiration, Jenny has also had two devotionals published in *The Upper Room* magazine and has written many other devotionals that she hopes to one day publish in book form. Jenny's blog, Liberty Ladies Devotional, is available at www.libertayladiesdevotional.blogspot.com. God has been opening doors for Jenny, and as long as He can use her, she hopes to be diligent. In her spare time, Jenny helps with the grandchildren, teaches piano lessons, plays in two bell choirs, and quilts.

Jeanetta R. Chrystie (p. 73) and her husband live in Springfield, Missouri where she works as a distance Assistant Professor of Business Administration at Southwest Minnesota State University.

Jeanetta enjoys writing and has published more than 800 articles in magazines such as *Christian History*, *Discipleship Journal*, and *Clubhouse*. Her 150 newspaper columns appeared in the *Northwest Christian Examiner*, and she has contributed to anthology books and textbooks since the 1970s.

Jeanetta, a firm believer in spiritual journaling and prayer journaling, teaches Sunday School and has a passion to write Bible studies and devotions. As a survivor of both polio (age 2) and cancer (age 22), she clings to God as her mainstay and seeks to fulfill His reasons for preserving her life. Learn more at www.ClearGlassView.com. Connect on Twitter:@ ClearGlassView, LinkedIn: Jeanetta-Chrystie, and Pinterest: Jchrystie.

Sharon Cook (p. 102) spent most of her life in California, happily moving with her husband to Arizona in 2006. Recently widowed, she is a mother of four, grandmother of seven, and great-grandmother of thirteen.

In between her obsessive quilting and reading, she is a speaker who gives destination lectures on cruise ships, presents her lecture series "Our Marvelous Brain," speaks at Christian Women's Connection, and teaches Bible studies. She is a writer and editor, her book, *Windows on the World*, is available on Amazon.com or Kindle. She is currently working with her sister, a mother of four handicapped daughters, on a book about their family life.

After forty years, Lin Daniels (p. 39) retired from teaching physical education — all but one year serving at the elementary-school level. She and her twin sister are avid golfers and especially enjoy playing as partners. As such they negotiate over which identical clothing to wear but choose one item (usually a hat) to be different. It is essential to zig and zag as teammates, so they have to remain slightly dissimilar.

Recently, Lin has found a passion for pickleball – a game similar to tennis but played on a smaller court while using a whiffle ball. Her other interests include writing Christian devotions, working with youth at church, and preaching — when offered the opportunity. Lin gives thanks to God for the depths of His love as well as all the "surprises" He has graciously bestowed on her.

Jorja Davis (p. 9) is an award-winning writer and poet. She has also been a classroom teacher, Sunday school teacher and coordinator, librarian, Kappa Phi (Christian women's collegiate club) sponsor, and early-learning-center and church-youth director. All this and more were enabled by her husband Bill's career moves during a twenty-six-year Air Force career, and only three moves in the twenty years since he retired. Jorja now marks the block "retired" on demographic surveys. Mostly that means waiting to see what God plans next.

Jorja is the oldest of three sisters all of whom love and care deeply for their mother — just turned 90 and suffering from dementia — and for one another as they each grow older.

An award-winning writer and poet, Jorja now marks the block "retired" on demographic surveys. Mostly that means waiting to see what God plans next.

Steven Duke (p. 41) retired from Allstate Insurance Company and also the Air Force Reserve. He now works as an accident investigator for a major law firm in Fort Walton Beach, Florida. Steve graduated from the University of West Florida with a B.A. and M.A. He is a member at Crosspoint Methodist Church in Niceville, Florida.

Steve has been blogging almost every day at "Steven Duke Today" on Facebook. Recently, he attended his first Christian writers' retreat and is a member of the Destin chapter of Word Weavers International. When he is not writing, he enjoys kayaking and playing disc golf. He is married and has four daughters and five grandchildren. He and his wife now love on three dogs, a Chihuahua, a Yorkie, and a Jack Russell Terrier.

Nicey T. Eller (p. 113) grew up in the Florida Panhandle and decided she wanted to be a writer. She received her B.A. in English from Shorter College, and her M.S. in Secondary Education and Ed.S. in Educational Leadership from Troy University.

When she retired as an elementary school principal, she traded her suits for boots, built a log home with her husband, and started a cattle ranch.

Her poetry, inspired by teachers, has been published in Teachers of Vision magazine. She was a co-author of *The Mighty Pen* (Christian Encouragement from Writers to Writers). She serves as a Sunday School teacher and leader in Celebrate Recovery. She is an avid reader, walker, and letter writer. Her contact information is nicey.eller123@gmail.com and facebook.com/nicey.eller.

Jacinta S. Fontenelle (p. 128) was born in the beautiful Caribbean island of St Lucia, and God has constantly demonstrated His love for her through many a difficult and challenging time. For over forty years she has worked as a nurse. She is currently working as an adjunct clinical instructor striving to motivate and inspire the next generation of nursing students.

Until recently, writing has been a hobby that encouraged and sustained her through the years. Now she is embarking on a second career as a poet/writer. She won first place for prose at the 2018 Greater Philadelphia Christian Writers Conference.

Her other hobbies have been reading, needlework and gardening. One of thirteen children, she values her family as one of God's greatest gifts to her. She strives to cherish that special gift as she lives in the state of Delaware, with her husband and three children.

Heidi Gaul (p. 43) lives in Oregon, where she leads a Bible Study Fellowship group. Winner of the 2015 Cascade Award for devotionals, her pieces can be found in several issues of *The Upper Room* in addition to two *Guideposts* devotionals, "Every Day with Jesus" and "Mornings with Jesus – 2019." Her stories are included in ten *Chicken Soup for the Soul* anthologies, and she's a staff writer for Good Catch Publishing, which distributes testimonial books to the unsaved.

Her current project is *Broken Dreams and Detours: When God's Will Doesn't Match Your Plans*. This book examines the myriad ways God works in our lives, bringing us closer to Him.

In her home garden, she lovingly cultivates a variety of flowering plants and enjoys travel — be it around the block or the world.

Pam Groupe Groves' (p. 47) childhood helped prepare her for writing, teaching and moving with her husband, Stan, from the Oregon high desert to the coast and finally to the big city. Their priority and joy in life was parenting six adopted children, four with special needs.

Stan met only two of their grandchildren before a rare cancer took his life at age 62. All five of the grandchildren know about Grandpa Stan and the childhoods of their parents from the many stories they must endure from Grandma Pam, their parents, aunts, uncles, and other relatives. The lives of the Groves family members continue to be a little offbeat with unexpected twists and turns. Through it all, trusting God has sustained them.

Sara Hague (p. 31) is a children's pastor, happy wife, and homeschooling mother of five talented children including one on the severe end of the Autism Spectrum. A life-long lover of learning, she spends her days brushing up on her Algebra and creating lessons for the children in her local church.

Since writing her own construction-paper and yarn-bound book of poetry in third grade, she has continued to hone her writing craft. Sara finds that shorter usually is sweeter, and fewer words chosen and fit together with care build a more satisfying story. She has published articles in *Focus on the Family Magazine, Clubhouse Jr., The Upper Room, Short and Sweet: Small Words for Big Thoughts,* and *Christian News Northwest.* Sara and her family enjoy exploring hiking trails, waterfalls, and coastal tide pools near their home in Central Oregon.

The blue-haired writer, Leah "LM" Hinton (p. 48), always has her nose in a book, whether she is reading it or writing it. She has been married to a big-city detective for over twenty years and lives in a suburb of Dallas, Texas. She and her husband have been blessed with two children, five rescue dogs, a bird, and a rescue horse — all named after her favorite characters in literature.

Leah writes both fiction and non-fiction and is fueled by highly caffeinated coffee and a never-ending faith in God. A country girl at heart, this homeschool mom and cancer wife loves sharing her struggles and blessings with others going through similar situations and firmly believes that faith is the best remedy for life's toils.

Paul Aaron Hinton (p. 20) is the son of a proper British mother and a Mississippi mud father. Never sure if he should aspire to be James Bond or a character from Hee Haw, Paul has worked in many "fields." He hopes his colorful — if not ADD — view of the world reaches those who have never been sure if God needs them. Thus, Paul's motto is Philippians 4:13: *I can do all things through Christ who strengthens me.*

Paul has served the Methodist church for over 20 years as a Lay Minister in both youth and contemporary worship. He and his wife, Cecily, have three children, plus a "Crazy Cat Lady" starter pack of four cats and two very big dogs.

Patricia Huey (p. 117) was born in the Pacific Northwest but was raised in the South. She began her teaching career after graduating from the University of Alabama. Throughout her career, the subject she most enjoyed teaching was creative writing. In 2015 she retired as director of Hill Creek Christian School in Mount Vernon, Washington — the school she founded in 1994. She serves as a consultant for Hill Creek Christian, offering educational therapy to students who struggle with learning deficits.

Currently Patricia is developing her writing ideas to point her readers to God. In her spare time, she enjoys gardening, writing, and bird watching outside by her pond. She also enjoys time spent with family, friends, and her two Labrador retrievers, Braveheart and Scout.

Charles Huff (p. 54) served as a Bible teacher and minister in his church for twenty years. He and his wife have traveled three times to the Philippines where they held pastors' seminars and taught in various churches.

He is a contributing author to James Stuart Bell's *Gifts from Heaven: True Stories of Miraculous Answers to Prayer* and his devotionals have been published at www.christiandevotions.us and *The Upper Room*. His Boosterclub blog at www.chashuff.wordpress.com offers encouragement toward the abundant life Jesus promised. He and his wife are charter members of Word Weavers International of Aurora, Illinois.

When not writing, Charles can be found out in nature with his camera or working on his list of chores and errands. He and his wife live in Aurora, Illinois, near their five children and six grandchildren.

Penny L. Hunt's (p. 56) greatest desire in life is to help others enter into a passionate relationship with Jesus Christ. She is an award-winning Amazon.com bestselling author, speaker, devotions writer, and also posts a weekly blog, "A Thought from Penny." The wife of a retired naval officer and attaché, Penny shares with warmth, motivation and humor the life lessons she has learned on a journey that has taken her from the east coast of the USA to Hawaii, Europe, South America and back.

Penny's adventure continues as a grateful grandma, happily living among the peach orchards of rural South Carolina with her husband Bill and Hunley, a rescue dog from the streets of Charleston. Penny is a prolific writer and member of Word Weavers International. Visit her at her website www.PennyL.Hunt.com.

In the summer of 2017, Tom Kennedy (p. 59) retired from Houston Baptist University as a professor of psychology and counseling. He taught marriage and family courses as well as human sexuality at the undergraduate level. In addition, he was the chair of the Master of Arts in Christian Counseling program where he taught Christian integration of Bible, theology, and counseling. Tom has been a Licensed Professional Counselor in Texas for almost thirty-five years. Due to hearing  loss, he has retired from face-to-face counseling but continues to work as an email suicide crisis counselor for Global Missions Online.

These days, Tom is busy playing with eight grandchildren and trying to start a writing career. Prior to his teaching at Houston Baptist University, Tom and his family were missionaries to Japan for fourteen years.

Liz Kimmel (p. 63) lives in St. Paul, Minnesota, has been married for 39 years, and is the mother of two and grandmother of four. She earned a BA in Elementary Education at Bethel College in Arden Hills, Minnesota.

Liz loves to write in such a way as to make learning fun for elementary students. She has published two books of Christian poetry and a grammar workbook. Her current project is a set of worksheets about the 50 U.S. states — created in order of  statehood and incorporating math and language arts skills, in addition to lots of puzzles. She serves as the Communications Coordinator for her church, Bethel Christian Fellowship, in St. Paul. Liz writes for and is layout editor for their bi-monthly church publication, and she currently serves as the communications coordinator for her church, Bethel Christian Fellowship, in St. Paul.

Susan Thogerson Maas (p. 66) lives in the beautiful state of Oregon and writes nonfiction for adults —mostly devotionals and personal-experience articles — and fiction for children, including a book for middle grade students, Picture Imperfect. Susan was a 2018 Cascades Awards Finalist in the category of Articles, Columns, and Blog Posts.

She also writes passages and questions for standardized tests, sadly the best-paying of her ventures. In her free time, Susan likes to go hiking and camping with her husband, take nature photographs, work in her vegetable garden, and travel — mainly to Tokyo, where one son and his wife live, and Pittsburgh, where the other son, his wife, and their two little boys live. She loves being a grandma.

Darlene S. Mackey (p. 68) is 70 years old, married to Dave for 50 years. They have one son and eleven grandchildren, ranging in ages from twelve to twenty-eight. Neither their son nor their grandchildren are biological, but they couldn't love them more.

Darlene has lived in Indiana, Northern Ireland, Rhode Island, Arizona, California, and now Tennessee. She has loved and loathed many things about all the places where she has lived. Darlene has worked as a dental assistant, a bookkeeper, and a church secretary. She is now happily retired.

Darlene and her husband have traveled to Paris, France; Nairobi, Kenya, and just recently, Israel. They love meeting people and learning about different cultures. Darlene has found that people are more alike than different and that the differences she does find are what make people delightfully special.

Angela Mattingly (p. 92) is a freelance writer who provides articles and devotions for books and magazines. In addition to being a writer, she is a photographer and painter. Her works are inspired by her faith and experiences as an accountant, business owner, teacher, and farmer. Twenty-two years of life on the farm, and experiences in hiking on trails from one end of the country to the other, provides lots of material for writing.

As a member of FaithWriters, she has won multiple writing contests. Some of these writings can be found on her website at www.treasuredglances.com along with her self-published devotions. She has photographs and pieces published in the 2014 and 2015 issues of Forces Literary Journal of the Arts. Her photos have won multiple awards and been chosen for a calendar publication.

Alice H. Murray (p. 84), a proud member of a military family, lives in Florida where she has practiced adoption law (domestic non-related infant adoptions) for over 25 years. Alice is an officer and board member of the Florida Adoption Council and of Hope Global Initiative.

While being a lawyer is her profession, Alice's passion is writing. Alice has written articles for legal professional magazines as well as for her local paper and a missions' magazine; she also won an American Bar Association haiku contest. Alice had a non-fiction piece published in Short and Sweet (the first book in the Short and Sweet series). In the near future, she hopes to have two books published — one a humorous devotional book and one a look back at her career as "Boss of the Babies" doing adoption work.

Kelly Pankratz (p. 132) is a Chicago native who followed her husband Paul to live in the Dakota Territory for, most likely, the rest of her life. They have been married twenty-two years and are raising four children and a labradoodle. On most days, the doodle is her favorite kid.

Kelly has a BA in Bible-Theology and an MA in Linguistics. She teaches high school English full-time and loves mentoring and empowering today's youth.

In her free time, Kelly likes to read, watch action movies, and travel. She is currently working on her second novel while pitching her first young-adult manuscript to agents. Find her at www.kellypankratz.com or on social media at www.facebook.com/kelly.pankratz, www.instagram.com/kellyapankratz, and www.twitter.com/kellypankratz.

Debra Pierce (p. 76) lives in Auburn, Massachusetts with her husband, David. She holds an Associate Degree in Animal Care from Becker College in Leicester, Massachusetts and a Bachelor of Arts degree in English from Worcester State College in Worcester, Massachusetts. Debra left a banking career to pursue her lifelong dream of working with animals. And in 1999, she started her pet-care business.

Debra is a voracious reader and enjoys writing devotionals, several of which have been published by The Upper Room. Her other interests are gardening, birdwatching, walks in the woods, and visiting museums. She was a volunteer for Mass Audubon, a wildlife volunteer at a nature/science museum, and most recently, ministry leader for her church's garden ministry. As Debra approaches retirement, she looks forward to traveling with her husband and devoting more time to her writing.

When not pent up writing in his office surrounded by old maps, petrified fossils, venerable tomes, and other dusty junk, Ken Proctor (p. 79) enjoys hiking and biking with his wife near their home in Vancouver, Washington, and exploring the rocky hills around Phoenix, Arizona, for stones and bones. And untold tales.

With a bachelor's degree and a master's degree — neither of which has anything to do with writing — Ken's creativity wells from his natural curiosity, extensive personal studies, and decades of observation. A semi-retired landscaper with an eye and ear for subtle detail, Ken crafts dioramas into his fiction, distinctive personalities into his characters, and memorable moments into their stories.

Frank Ramirez (p. 91) shares three adult children and six grandchildren with Jennie, his spouse of 43 years. They share their home with three dogs. Frank was born in California, but as a Navy Brat his childhood was spent in several states all over the country. He graduated from LaVerne College in California and from Bethany Theological Seminary, which at the time was located near Chicago. Since then he has been a pastor in the Church of the Brethren since 1979, serving churches in California, Indiana, and Pennsylvania.

Frank is also a prolific writer, an avid reader, and a beekeeper. His favorite authors include William Shakespeare, J.R.R. Tolkien, Rex Stout, C.S. Lewis, Samuel Beckett, and Saki. He owns two much-used editions of the Oxford English Dictionary. He reads Biblical Hebrew and Greek. Frank lives near Nappanee, Indiana.

Michael Reynolds (p. 71) is a graduate of Bethel College, and Asbury Theological Seminary and is an ordained minister in the Missionary Church. He first served the denomination in curriculum development and distribution, then pastored for five years. He became editor of his denomination's magazine, *Emphasis on Faith and Living*, then joined the overseas department, known as World Partners, serving for 21 years as coordinator of media. His duties included writing, editing, and graphic design for in-house publications; developing video projects; maintaining websites; and providing technical support for staff.

He is retired and enjoys writing, teaching adult Sunday School, fishing, and doing handyman projects for friends and family. He and his wife Sherri live in Zanesville Indiana.

Reba Rhyne (p. 12) is the pen name of Reba Carolyn Rhyne Meiller. She was raised in the western foothills of the Great Smoky Mountains, where her roots are firmly established.

Three-quarters of a century have passed since she was born. During this time, she was married for twenty-five years, had a daughter, and established a business as an on-site consultant, prototyping upholstered interiors for the marine industry. During her months on the road, she decided to write one-sheets about her travels. After attending several writing conferences, she expanded her scribbling. Her first novel, *Butterfield Station*, is available at Amazon, your local bookstore or Kindle.

For sixty years, she's been a Christ-follower who believes her responsibility is to follow the Great Commission found in Matthew. Contact her at rebarhyne@gmail.com.

After graduating from local schools and the University of Redlands, Susanna (p. 87) married Robert L. Robar. Robert, a retired Los Angeles City fire captain, and Susanna, a retired Spanish teacher, have five children: two children are with the Lord; three adult children and four grandchildren live in Southern California.

Through her ministries, RapeSpeaksOut!, Susanna uses written materials, workshops, seminars, and short-term courses to educate parents, teachers, pastors, and other child caregivers about sexual violence, child safety, and human-sex trafficking. Her purpose is to help heal victims of sexual violence and prevent more children from becoming such victims.

For her efforts, Susanna received the InauguralCottey College Alumnae Hall of Leadership and Social Responsibility Award.

After dabbling in several careers throughout her adult life, Dottie Rogers (p. 136) is now happily retired. She is a graduate of Huntingdon College, Scarritt College, and the University of South Alabama. She was blessed to spend twenty years in the areas of local church Christian education and university campus ministry. She then had many rewarding years as a professional counselor in several settings.

She now enjoys hanging around the house with her husband Ken and their dog Shep. They live near the gulf coast where gardening is a twelve-month project. She also loves to read, cook, write, and teach adult Bible study. After fifty years of discipleship, she is still learning to follow. Although a reluctant disciple, she is always amazed at God's grace and guidance.

In 2003, Pamela Rosales (p. 97) joined a writing group and then Oregon Christian Writers shortly thereafter. She began writing freelance and her articles, poems, and devotions have been published in several Christian publications since 2004. Some of the publications include: *The Secret Place* and *God's Word For Today* devotionals; "Live," a Gospel Publishing House leaflet; June Cotner's poetry anthology books; and *Imago Dei* magazine.

Pamela has worked as an administrative assistant in public schools, in her church, and as administrator for her husband's court-reporting business. She has also served in various leadership roles in her church and as a women's Bible study leader. She and her husband have entered a new phase of life and now spend retirement half their time in Oregon and the other half in southern California.

Toni Armstrong Sample (p. 34) retired early to Greenwood, South Carolina at the end of a successful career as a human-resource executive. She has written for professional journals, recreational magazines, devotionals, newspapers, and inspirational-story publications. Her first novel, *The Glass Divider*, was released in 2014 followed in 2015 and 2016 with *Transparent Web of Dreams*, *Distortion*, and *A Still Small Voice*.

Toni is a Christian retreat leader and conference speaker, Christian education and women's Bible study facilitator and commission artist — concentrating on painting Biblical scenes and characters. Her first non-fiction book, *I'll Never be the Same*, was released in 2017. Her second non-fiction book is titled *A Buck Three Eighty (A Baby-Boomers Stories About Growing Up in the North)*. She also has inspirational stories published in the *Divine Moments* series.

Laura Luptowski Seeley (p. 37) is a Michigan-based freelance writer and editor with more than 35 years of experience. She held various writing and editing positions at Michigan State University in East Lansing for nearly 27 years prior to establishing Classic Writing & Editing Services, LLC in 2013. Her work has appeared in numerous newsletters, magazines, newspapers, and other publications over the years, including the premier magazine of the horse industry — *Equus*. For several years she also wrote a monthly humor column for *Arabian Horse Express*.

Recently she founded The Cat Ambassador, Inc., a nonprofit organization that provides financial assistance for cat owners so they can afford to keep their pets, rather than relinquish them to an animal shelter. She and her husband, Harley, live in Haslett, Michigan, with several cats of their own.

David Alan Shorts (p. 95) is a writer, speaker, and musician from Lodi, California. A graduate of San Jose State's school of music, he has spent the last 18 years teaching elementary music and band.

When he's not being a daddy to his three incredible children, he speaks at a convalescent hospital, snow skis, and flies model airplanes.

David wrote his first story, Melido's Blade, in sixth grade. In high school he switched to musician mode and pursued a career, playing at local venues and writing many songs and a few musicals. He released two albums under the names *Strohsdivad* and *Dead Poet Clan*.

For the last ten years he has written many YA novels, screen plays, and children's stories. This year he added flash fiction and devotional writing. Visit his web page at www.facebook.com/DavidAlanShorts.

Long-time Bible student and teacher, Lisa Worthey Smith (p. 52), finds that God often reveals profound truths in ordinary events. Her use of those simple events to explain biblical truths led to her being called The Parable Teacher. Both her teaching and writings reflect a deep faith and passion to help others know God and see Him at work in their lives.

She and her husband live in north Alabama where she writes stories of finding evidence of the hand of God all around us in everyday events, especially wildlife she observes in her own backyard. Her desire is to have daily COFFEE with God (Consecration, Obedience, and Fearless Faith in Everything Every day).

You can read more stories of faith on her blog LifeInMyFathersWorld. blogspot.com and find her books on Amazon.com.

Writer and illustrator E.V. Sparrow (p. 104) enjoys spending time with her new husband and young grandchildren and serving as caretaker for her mother. Her favorite activities are hiking, kayaking, and creating art. During her years as a muralist, E.V. loved painting whimsical designs in children's rooms. Her current illustration projects, in watercolor and pen, depict the joy of life and relationships.

Prayer, worship, and ministry are vital to E.V. She led prayer teams and small groups in Divorce Care, Women's, and Singles' Ministries; and sang with a worship team and several choirs. E.V. served on short-term mission trips and lived abroad.

E.V. is a member of Inspire Christian Writers and the Society of Children's Book Writers and Illustrators. Her passion is writing short stories of freedom, hope, and love. Her favorite subjects are interpersonal relationships and God's miraculous interactions with His people.

Randy Swanson (p. 108), retired attorney, trumpet professional, Bible teacher, and world traveler to over 75 countries, has self-published a 600-page travelogue, *Visiting the World*, about his 2-year adventure in his VW Camper. He has written articles for *Charisma Magazine* and *Christianity Today*, has written a regular column for *Significant Living Magazine*, and has written for *The Upper Room*.

Randy serves on numerous nonprofit boards in the United States, such as Worship Leader Foundation, Forever Kids, Warehouse Ministries, Azure Arts Foundation, New Life Christian Center Church and China Mercy. He is a voracious reader and a theatrical movie and documentary enthusiast. Randy is married to Samantha Landy, an international radio host with her program "Psalms of Hope." Randy continues to play his trumpet in numerous bands and brass groups and is working on a new novel entitled *The Trumpet Player*.

Jewell Utt (p. 25) is a freelance writer and conference speaker. Her passion is to encourage women through the Word of God. Understanding the demands of life, she presents retreats that promote rest, change, and renewal. "Refreshment for the Servant's Heart" is one of her popular retreat themes. Jewell considers seeing women revived for their journey to be a great reward.

For over twenty years, Jewell has served in church leadership with a focus on teaching and outreach. She is the director of a community food pantry and the women's-ministry leader at her church. She and her husband live in a serene mountainous area. They have three married sons and enjoy playing with their first grandson. To read her devotions or book a retreat, visit her website at: www.jewellutt.com.

Mary Hunt Webb (p. 126) is a recovering educator with a master's degree in adult education and workplace training and a bachelor's degree in Spanish. Her recovery is not going well since she teaches American Sign Language and supervises volunteers at her church. Because she is skilled in making difficult subjects understandable to audiences of varying abilities, Mary has taught Spanish, English as a Second Language, and math. She specialized in assisting students to overcome life's challenges and attain career goals.

In order to reach those outside the classroom, Mary has written for various secular and Christian publications, including *Woman's Day* and *The Upper Room*. She was a professional consultant for *The Art of Helping* and for *Love Extravagantly*. Mary and her husband own a consulting firm, Heart Works. Her husband is the webmaster for their website, www.maryhuntwebb.com.

Kenneth Avon White (p. 121) is an aspiring writer whose first publishing credit was for a devotional in *The Upper Room* magazine. He is also published in the first three books of the *Short & Sweet* series. Ken's professional background includes radio and television advertising, public relations, and corporate communications. He dreams of making writing his career; but in the meantime, he is grateful for the clock he punches.

For years, Ken lived in Nashville, Tennessee where he enjoyed the local music scene, theatrical shows, and art exhibits. Also high on his list there was dining out with a cast of characters — otherwise known as close friends — who have all been warned that most likely they will find themselves in one of his stories someday. Recently, he left Nashville to start a new job in Charlotte, North Carolina.

Andrea Woronick (p. 82) lives in New England with her husband, Michael, and her dog Rupert. She received a master's degree in biology and worked in medical research for several years until her two children were born.

At that time, she chose to stay home to raise her children and then began volunteering at their schools and in her church. For fifteen years she worked as the Director of Faith Formation at her church — creating, overseeing, and teaching programs for children and adults. She has since resigned her position and spends her time volunteering at a non-profit medical children's charity and at her church.

Andrea enjoys playing the piano, reading, gardening, traveling, and taking long walks with Rupert. She loves to write and hopes to continue to pursue this passion.

CPSIA information can be obtained
at www.ICGtesting.com
Printed in the USA
BVHW020610021218
534357BV00012B/82/P